Continuity *and* Change

Three Generations of Ethiopian Artists

Rebecca Martin Nagy

with essays by
Achamyeleh Debela
Heran Sereke-Brhan
Shiferaw Bekele
Geta Mekonnen
Leah Niederstadt

Samuel P. Harn Museum of Art

University of Florida
Gainesville, Florida

Continuity and Change:
Three Generations of Ethiopian Artists

Samuel P. Harn Museum of Art
University of Florida, Gainesville, Florida
January 23, 2007 - April 29, 2007

Diggs Gallery of Winston-Salem State University
Winston-Salem, North Carolina
May 26, 2007 - December 8, 2007

Library of Congress Cataloging-in-Publication Data

Continuity and change : three generations of Ethiopian artists.
       p. cm.
Issued in connection with an exhibition held Jan. 23-Apr. 29, 2007, Samuel P. Harn Museum of Art, University of Florida, Gainesville.
Includes bibliographical references.
ISBN 978-0-9762552-3-9
1. Art, Ethiopian—Ethiopia—Addis Ababa—20th century—Exhibitions.
2. Art and state—Ethiopia—History—20th century—Exhibitions. I. Samuel P. Harn Museum of Art.

N7386.C67 2007
709.63'07475979—dc22

                                                                                          2006102534

Editing: Christine Hale
Design and Production: Tami Wroath and Christine Hale
Photography: David Blankenship

cover:
Lulseged Retta
Jazz Night (Tribute to Gebre Kristos Desta), 1993
Acrylic on cotton cloth on board
59 1/4 x 29 3/4 in. (150.5 x 75.6 cm.)
Collection of the artist

back cover:
Geta Mekonnen
The Hands, 2005
Oil and acrylic on canvas
Each panel 39 1/4 x 31 1/2 in. (99.7 x 80 cm.)
Collection of the artist

Contents

Artist Entries

Rebecca Martin Nagy

Achamyeleh (Acha) Debela and I began our dialogue about contemporary Ethiopian art in 1998 when the North Carolina Museum of Art in Raleigh, where I was then a curator, acquired Skunder Boghossian's 1964 painting *Night Flight of Dread and Delight*. It was fortuitous for me that Acha, a former student and close friend of Skunder's, was a professor at nearby North Carolina Central University in Durham. Our conversations about Skunder and his contemporaries soon inspired us to plan an exhibition of Ethiopian art that would put Skunder's work into a broader cultural and art historical context for American audiences. When I moved to Gainesville, Florida to become director of the Samuel P. Harn Museum of Art at the University of Florida in 2002, we continued our research with the goal of opening the exhibition at the Harn Museum of Art in 2007. We are delighted that *Continuity and Change: Three Generations of Ethiopian Artists* will also have a North Carolina venue at the Diggs Gallery of Winston-Salem State University, where our friend and colleague Belinda Tate is director. I am grateful to my colleagues at the North Carolina Museum of Art who encouraged and supported the early stages of research for this project, especially Director Lawrence J. Wheeler and then-Chief Curator John W. Coffey.

Beginning in 2001, Acha and I made six research trips to Ethiopia and with each amazing journey I learned to love more deeply the country, its people and its vibrant artistic traditions. For Acha each trip was a homecoming. He grew up in Addis Ababa, studied at the Addis Ababa Fine Arts School and experienced firsthand the "Addis Spring" of the 1960s in the last years of Emperor Haile Selassie's reign. From his studies abroad in Nigeria and the United States, he witnessed the unfolding in Ethiopia of the 1974 Revolution and the seventeen-year rule of the authoritarian Derg regime under Mengistu Haile Mariam. Following the lives and careers of his former teachers and fellow students at the Addis Ababa Fine Arts School, he always maintained a strong connection to the school. After the overthrow of the Derg in 1991, Acha returned to Ethiopia as a Fulbright scholar to advise the administration and faculty of the School of Fine Arts as it became a department of Addis Ababa University with refurbished facilities, a new curriculum and a new name, the School of Fine Arts and Design (SFAD). Because of Acha's professional relationships and enduring friendships in Ethiopia, I have been received with open arms and gracious hospitality at the SFAD and in the studios and homes of artists in Addis Ababa. I am deeply grateful to Acha Debela, co-curator of this exhibition, for sharing with me his deep knowledge and great love of Ethiopian modern and contemporary art. This exhibition is the result of a collaborative partnership and would not have been possible without Acha's enthusiastic participation and passionate commitment over almost a decade.

Of the twenty-three artists included in *Continuity and Change: Three Generations of Ethiopian Artists*, only three are deceased—Agegnehu Engida, Gebre Kristos Desta and Skunder Boghossian. The other twenty artists live and work in and near Addis Ababa, a cosmopolitan city with a lively arts community, home to many interesting and noteworthy artists whose work is still largely unknown outside Ethiopia and a small circle of international scholars, curators and collectors. As Acha and I defined the scope of the exhibition, we decided not to include the work of contemporary artists living in the Diaspora, in part because their work is already better known to European and American audiences. We chose to focus on the role of the School of Fine Arts and Design in Addis Ababa, one of Africa's premier art academies, which has shaped and influenced the careers of three generations of Ethiopian artists and which also has been shaped by the changing political climate in Ethiopia. The school's founder, Ale Felege Selam Heruy, and early instructors at the school, including Gebre Kristos Desta and Skunder Boghossian, taught and nurtured, with the support of Emperor Haile Selassie, a group of artists who are at mid-career today. Among those second-generation artists who worked during the Marxist Derg regime are Yohannes Gedamu, Lulseged

Retta and Desta Hagos, independent painters living from the sale of their work. Also among the second-generation of contemporary artists are teachers at the SFAD, including Zerihun Yetmgeta, Mezgebu Tessema and several others. Their students are the third generation of artists in the exhibition, recent graduates of the school such as Elias Sime, Tamrat Gezahegne and Tesfahun Kibru, who have worked in relative freedom since the overthrow of Mengistu's government in 1991.

In contrast to many contemporary artists in other parts of the world, most Ethiopian artists choose painting as their principal medium, and the overwhelming majority of works in the current exhibition are paintings. Among the artists we selected for the show, only Bekele Mekonnen and his former student Tesfahun Kibru focus primarily on sculpture, whereas Elias Sime works in a variety of media including sculpture, collage, embroidery and assemblage. The emphasis on painting in modern and contemporary Ethiopian art relates to the importance of painting in the history of the Ethiopian Orthodox Church since medieval times, when illustrated manuscripts, icons and mural paintings were first produced by church artists for use in religious observance. Sculpture was never a major medium of church art, and it was from church art that secular painting developed in the nineteenth and twentieth centuries. Secular painting gave rise in due course to modern and contemporary art, in large measure because of the patronage of Emperor Haile Selassie, who championed modern art as part of his campaign to modernize Ethiopia and bring the country into closer political, economic and social contact with the outside world. Most of the first and second generation artists included in this exhibition have studied and traveled in Africa, Europe and North America and have experienced at least limited exposure to international contemporary forms of artistic expression, including the alternate media prevalent in Western countries. Nonetheless, most artists in Addis Ababa today continue to embrace painting as their preferred medium. We hope that

American audiences will approach their work with openness to a different world view, one rooted in Ethiopia's ancient and distinctive cultural heritage yet shaped by exposure to and interest in the artistic expression of other regions of Africa and the world.

Rebecca Martin Nagy

In 2003, thanks to a consultation grant from the National Endowment for the Humanities, a group of scholars came together at the Harn Museum of Art to help conceptualize and define the nature of a proposed exhibition of Ethiopian art and its related publication and programs. Their enthusiastic support, sage advice and creative ideas contributed greatly to our thinking about the project. For their contributions at an early stage in the planning process, Achamyeleh (Acha) Debela and I extend our sincere thanks to Steven Brandt of the University of Florida; Ian Campbell, an independent scholar from Washington, D.C.; Richard Pankhurst of the Institute of Ethiopian Studies at Addis Ababa University; Steven Kaplan of Hebrew University; Betsy Quick of the Fowler Museum of Cultural History at the University of California, Los Angeles; Kay Kaufman Shelemay of Harvard University; and Raymond A. Silverman of the University of Michigan.

So many individuals in Ethiopia have assisted us in a variety of ways that it is impossible to thank each of them here. Among the first and most enthusiastic supporters of our project was Hapte-Selassie Tafesse, former Minister of Tourism of Ethiopia, to whom we will always be deeply grateful for all that he has done to smooth our way. Another steadfast consultant and facilitator throughout the project was Besufekad Debela, whose boundless energy and endless resourcefulness made possible the seemingly impossible. In addition to their contributions to the catalogue, both Heran Sereke-Brhan and Geta Mekonnen have contributed immeasurably to development of the exhibition in other ways. Our friend Worku Sharew has also kindly assisted us over the years.

We are especially grateful to the artists who have generously shared their experiences and insights and made their work available for the exhibition, and to other lenders who agreed to part with cherished works of art. Their names appear elsewhere in the catalogue. Acha and I owe a special debt to our esteemed colleagues who have contributed essays for the catalogue: Heran Sereke-Brhan, Shiferaw Bekele, Geta Mekonnen and Leah Niederstadt. Their distinctive voices greatly enrich the discourse on modern and contemporary Ethiopian art and their passionate yet exacting scholarship makes an enduring contribution to the field. Ambassador Mohamoud Dirir, Minister of Culture and Tourism, and Jara Haile Mariam, General Manager of the Authority for Research and Conservation of Cultural Heritage, graciously extended their support of the exhibition. At the National Museum of Ethiopia, Director Mamitu Yilma and Curator Aynalem Emiru kindly and enthusiastically gave their assistance, and at the Institute of Ethiopian Studies, Director Elizabeth Wolde Giorgis and Curator Ahmed Zekaria offered help and advice along the way. We gratefully acknowledge their support and assistance. Others who shared their knowledge and insights and to whom we owe thanks are Muzie Awol, director of the School of Fine Arts and Design; Konjit Seyoum, director of Asni Gallery; architect Fasil Giorgis; filmmaker Salem Mekuria; and anthropologist and independent curator Meskerem Assegued. I also extend thanks to colleagues in Europe, Elisabeth Biasio at the Völkerkundemuseum of the University of Zurich and Girma Fisseha at the Staatliches Museum für Völkerkunde in Munich, for their kind assistance with research for the exhibition.

At the University of Florida and the Harn Museum of Art a number of individuals have contributed to the successful realization of the exhibition and catalogue. I have been privileged to have three outstanding art history graduate students as research interns during preparation of the exhibition and I am grateful to them: Kristen Flierl, Jaime Baird and Nicholas Frech. Former Registrar Mary Margaret Carr, Registrar Laura Nemmers and Associate Registrar Reagan Duplisea have been stalwart in their attention to the myriad of details associated with an international loan exhibition. Preparators Michael Peyton and Tim

Joiner ensured that the installation would be of the highest quality. Graphic designer Tami Wroath is responsible for the handsome catalogue design. Christine Hale's sharp editorial eye improved the publication in numerous ways. The one person who probably worked even harder on the exhibition than Acha or I is my incomparable assistant Coral Stimac. I can never thank her enough.

At the Harn Museum, *Continuity and Change: Three Generations of Ethiopian Artists* is accompanied by a corollary exhibition in an adjacent gallery titled *Art of the Ethiopian Highlands from the Harn Museum Collection*, made possible by generous support from The C. Frederick and Aase B. Thompson Foundation. I am indebted and thankful to art historian Marilyn Heldman for enthusiastically sharing her expertise with Harn Curator of African Art Susan Cooksey, graduate intern Nicholas Frech and myself as we examined works from the museum's collection in preparing for this installation.

For essential support of research and development of the exhibition I gratefully acknowledge the National Endowment for the Humanities and the Fine Arts Scholarship Enhancement Fund of the University of Florida's College of Fine Arts. The exhibition and catalogue are made possible through the generous support of the University of Florida, private foundations, corporations and individuals. I am especially grateful to Northern Trust Bank as major exhibition sponsor. The exhibition is also made possible by support from the Harn Museum's Margaret J. Early Program Endowment, Harn Program Endowment and 150th Anniversary Cultural Plaza Endowment, and the State of Florida Division of Cultural Affairs. For support of the catalogue I extend deepest gratitude to Dr. Madelyn Lockhart and The C. Frederick and Aase B. Thompson Foundation. Additional major support for the catalogue has been provided by the Harn Museum of Art's John Early Publications Endowment and the University of Florida Office of Graduate Research. In addition, for their contributions to support this publication I sincerely thank Drs. Jane and Gerald Katcher of Miami; Carolyn and Sandy Stidham of Raleigh; and other North Carolina friends—Edith Klemstine, Connie Shertz, Jane Steele, Karin Vander Elst and Sarah Almblad.

Educational programming in conjunction with the exhibition is made possible by generous support from the Harn Eminent Scholar Endowment of the School of Art and Art History, College of Fine Arts, University of Florida; the International Center, University of Florida; and the Center for African Studies, University of Florida.

Achamyeleh Debela is professor of art at North Carolina Central University (NCCU) in Durham, North Carolina. He is a graduate of the Addis Ababa Fine Arts School and Ahmadu Bello University in Zaria, Nigeria; holds advanced degrees from Morgan State University and the Maryland Institute of Art; and did doctoral studies at Ohio State University in art education and computer graphics. He is a two-time recipient of the Teaching Excellence award from NCCU and was a Fulbright fellow in Ghana and Ethiopia from 2000 to 2002. He has published scholarly articles and book chapters on Ethiopian modern and contemporary art. He was one of ten artists whose work was included in the exhibition *Ethiopian Passages: Contemporary Art from the Diaspora* at the National Museum of African Art, Smithsonian Institution, in 2003.

Education in Ethiopia

Schooling of children in the Christian highlands of Ethiopia was historically conducted by the clergy and restricted almost exclusively to boys. The majority of pupils were drawn from the surrounding community. A father who happened to be a member of the clergy taught his sons, and the sons of church members attended the local church school. Sons of the aristocracy also received some church education, either privately or alongside the children of peasants. The main thrust of the curriculum was learning to read and recite religious texts written in the ancient liturgical language of Ge`ez. Not all pupils learned to write. Whereas most pupils did not persevere with their studies, true mastery of advanced learning in the Ethiopian Orthodox Church required thirty years of intensive study and scholarship.

Toward the end of the nineteenth century, Emperor Menilek II permitted the establishment of European missionary schools in Ethiopia. At the same time, Islamic schools provided some education for a small part of the Muslim population. By the beginning of the twentieth century, the education system's failure to meet the needs of people involved in statecraft, diplomacy, commerce and industry led to the introduction of government-sponsored secular education. The first public school, Menilek II School, was established in the capital city of Addis Ababa in 1907/08, and a year later a primary school opened in the eastern Ethiopian city of Harar. At this time many subjects in the schools were taught in French, the *lingua franca* of the Ethiopian intelligentsia. After 1941 English would supersede French as the preferred language of intellectual discourse and for instruction in the schools.[1]

In 1925 the government adopted a plan to expand secular education, but only limited progress was made toward this goal before the schools were closed during the Italian Fascist occupation of Ethiopia from 1936 to 1941. With the restoration of Ethiopian independence in 1941, primary schools reopened and the first secondary schools were established. The school system still faced many obstacles, including shortages of teachers, textbooks and facilities.

In 1961 Ethiopia hosted the United Nations-sponsored Conference of African States on the Development of Education in Africa. Among other things, the conference highlighted Ethiopia's educational deficiencies. The Ethiopian education system, especially in primary and secondary education, was ranked at the bottom among African nations. Embarrassed by this record, the Ministry of Education developed a new education policy, which gave precedence to the establishment of technical training schools, although academic education also was expanded. Curriculum revisions introduced a mix of academic and nonacademic subjects with Amharic as the language of instruction for the entire primary cycle. Under the revised system, two-year junior secondary schools offered a general academic program for individuals who wished to continue their education at technical or vocational schools or at four-year senior secondary schools. The curriculum at the senior secondary schools prepared students for intermediate positions in the civil service, armed forces or private enterprises or for higher education in Ethiopia or abroad.

By the 1950s Ethiopian students had two options for more advanced academic studies. The University College of Addis Ababa was established in 1950 with the stated mission "to provide the youth of Ethiopia with a sound academic background in the fields of Arts and Sciences, leading to further professional studies abroad."[2] Subsequently the name of the university was changed to Haile Selassie I University (1961-74) and then Addis Ababa University (1974 to the present). In 1954 a Roman Catholic religious order based in Italy founded the private University of Asmara. Today Asmara is the capital of Eritrea, which won its independence from Ethiopia in 1993.

Funding remained inadequate despite the fact that money spent on education increased from ten percent of total government expenditures in 1968 to twenty percent in the early 1970s. The imperial government, under the pressure of growing public dissatisfaction and mounting student activism in the secondary schools and university, initiated a comprehensive study of the education system. The Education Sector Review (ESR), completed in July 1972, recommended attaining universal primary education as quickly as possible, equalizing educational opportunities, and relating the entire system to the national development process. The ESR criticized the education system's focus on preparing students for the next level of academic study and on the completion of rigid qualifying examinations. Also criticized was the government's lack of concern for young people who dropped out before learning marketable skills, a situation that contributed to unemployment.

The report was not published until February 1974, which gave time for rumors to generate opposition to the ESR recommendations among students, parents and the teachers' union. Most resented what they considered the removal of education from its elite position. Many teachers also feared salary reductions. Strikes and widespread disturbances ensued, and the education crisis became a contributing factor in the imperial regime's fall later that year.[3]

Art and Artists in the Service of the Church

The function of church art in the Ethiopian highlands was the promotion and spreading of the Christian faith by forming and raising religious consciousness among believers, the majority of whom were illiterate. Art served to educate the masses at the same time it delighted the privileged sensibilities of the cultivated elite.

After completing his training at a church school, the artist became a lay cleric known as a *debtera* and worked anonymously as a craftsman in the service of the church. He shared the religious convictions that the church and the faithful expected him to express in his paintings. This does not mean that the artist did not change some forms, perhaps going against accepted dogma with regard to certain ways of depicting the Madonna and Child or the Crucifixion, for example. Rather, it means that his art had very little to do with any aspects of life outside of the religious one.

Early Ethiopian painters initially depicted figures and events of the Old and New Testaments and then the stories of the saints (fig. 1). It was not until the beginning of the eighteenth century that kings and nobility started to appear on the same stage with biblical figures and saints. In the nineteenth and twentieth centuries, patronage of emperors and nobility increased so that the church was no longer the sole or primary patron of artists. The new patrons appreciated art as a means of affirming their social prestige and artists came to depend on them for material existence. This was especially evident during the reign of Emperor Haile Selassie (1930-1974).[4] Portraits and murals depicting him as King of Kings, Elect of God and Lion of the Tribe of Judah prominently appeared in and around the churches of Addis Ababa and elsewhere on public buildings where visibility by proxy was deemed useful.

The Modern Era in the Arts and Some of the First Artists to Study Abroad

The Ethiopian modern era began in the early 1900s with the introduction of modern education. Prior to that, emperors sent a few individuals abroad for training so that they could assume positions of importance in the administration of the government. Modern education was understood as a means to an end, training for state employment.

In the 1920s a number of the Ethiopian intelligentsia returned home from abroad to

Fig. 1   *Diptych with the Virgin and Child, Saints and Scenes of the Passion and Resurrection of Christ*, Ethiopia
Late 17th to early 18th century
Tempera on gesso-covered wood panels
12 1/4 x 17 in. (31.1 x 43.2 cm.)
Partial gift of Richard Faletti and Museum purchase, funds provided by the Caroline Julier and James G. Richardson Acquisition Endowment, Michael A. Singer, and the David A. Cofrin Exhibition and Acquisition Endowment
Collection of the Samuel P. Harn Museum of Art
. 2003.10.13

of young Ethiopians in the mastery of the limited vocabulary of pidgin-Italian that employs only the infinitive of verbs among other incites, so that the fascist masters will have an efficient cook, dishwasher, or general servant unable to read serious books in the proper Italian language. On top of that, fascist censorship allowed only sycophantic literature and pro Italian political propaganda to appear in Amharic and ruthlessly scathed the faintest stirring of patriotic writing in the bud.[6]

Sculptor Abebe Wolde Giorgis (1897-1967) and painter Agegnehu Engida (1905-1950) were pioneering artists who studied in Europe in the early twentieth century. Around 1940 Abebe Wolde Giorgis returned home after eighteen years in Paris and Marseilles studying and working as a sculptor. Following his return, he received commissions for sculptures for the former Parliament Building, the Addis Ababa Municipality, the Menilek School, and at the Addis Alem Church.[7]

Agegnehu Engida was an accomplished painter who studied at the Ecole des Beaux-Arts in Paris from 1926 to 1933 (fig. 2). Among his few extant works is a self portrait in the collection of the National Museum of Ethiopia in Addis Ababa. Agegnehu's self portrait introduces the artist as a subject in contradistinction to the traditional anonymity of the *debtera* artist. The *debtera* did not sign his painting let alone introduce his own portrait into a religious image, although he did include portraits of his patrons.

To fulfill the government's mandate for cultural and artistic instruction in the schools, some handicraft classes were offered. Art classes were taught at only a handful of elite public schools such as General Wingate, Tafari Makonnen, Haile Selassie I Secondary School (Kotebe) and Menilek. In the mid-twentieth century there were only two individuals who taught the subject, namely Negadras Zerihun Dominico at Tafari Makonnen School and Shimeles Kabtimer at the Menilek School. In 1941 the Ministry of Education and Fine Arts officially acknowledged the importance of art in the education of children, establishing a Department of Fine Arts.[8] Sculptor Abebe Wolde Giorgis was its first administrator and painter Agegnehu Engida its assistant director. Other

contribute to the development of their society. They were eager propagandists for the modernizing line prescribed by the Regent and Emperor in the face of entrenched opposition from the clergy, the feudal elite and the uneducated masses.[5] They began to grapple with a number of issues concerning religion, education, practical ethics and the history of Ethiopia and her monarchs. With the added impetus of a new printing press, the first in the capital city, numerous volumes of poetry, prose, fiction and other writings were published. The invasion of Ethiopia by Fascist Italy in 1936 ended the budding intellectual output. Mengistu Lemma, in his article "Modern Amharic Literature: The Task Ahead," gives the following account of the systematic elimination of the Ethiopian intelligentsia:

> The Italian fascist dictatorship systematically exterminated members of the Ethiopian intelligentsia who had acquired their modern education in Europe. It confiscated and made bon-fires of books written in French or in English and proceeded to implement the South African Policy of apartheid in education, that coaxed Ethiopians to attend Italian schools but forced them to 'graduate' from the third elementary grade. The result aimed at by this policy was the training

personnel in the department included artists of prominence in the traditional folk art genre that had evolved from church painting in the late nineteenth and early twentieth centuries. They were given studio spaces at the old Parliament Building and were asked to create portraits of the royal family from photographs as well as other popular themes. Most of their paintings were distributed to government schools and offices or used as gifts for foreign dignitaries. Some of the artists were called upon to paint murals in churches and prominent government buildings.[9]

According to one source, Agegnehu Engida opened an informal art school with fourteen students in 1941 and Abebe Wolde Giorgis left his administrative duties at the Department of Fine Arts in 1956 to set up another art school at Arat Kilo near the Menilek School compound.[10] Although neither Abebe Wolde Giorgis or Agegnehu Engida succeeded in establishing an enduring art school, each took under his wings a few apprentices who were later to practice independently and even receive acclaim. Perhaps these small but important beginnings formed the foundation of what later became the Addis Ababa Fine Arts School in 1957/58.

By the 1950s many African nations were breaking free of the yoke of colonialism and the newly independent nations were building their infrastructures with all the resources available to them. Art played a major role in signifying and symbolically representing the meaning of nationhood, independence, the history of the colonial legacy and the new dreams and aspirations of the people. Artists were called upon to illustrate these ideas from the well of a rich and vast heritage, and many pan-Africanist artists were in the forefront in the creation and celebration of the independence of their nations. In Ethiopia painter and sculptor Afewerk Tekle made a significant contribution with his monumental stained glass window titled *The Struggle and Aspiration of the African People* executed from 1959-1961 for Africa Hall, the headquarters of the United Nations Economic Commission for Africa.

Afewerk received a government scholarship to study in England in 1947 and graduated with a degree in fine arts from the Slade School of Fine Art at the University of London in 1954. The modern artist best known to the majority of Ethiopians today, Afewerk still works at his imposing Addis Ababa home and studio, Villa Alpha. Having enjoyed the patronage of three successive Ethiopian governments, wide recognition at home and abroad, and corresponding financial success, Afewerk is credited with introducing into Ethiopian society a new appreciation of the artist as an educated professional who moves as an equal among academics and social and political elites. Although he did not teach at the Fine Arts School and never took students or apprentices, Afewerk is viewed as a role model by many artists who aspire to achieve professional acclaim and financial independence.

The Birth of the Addis Ababa Fine Arts School

The birth of the Addis Ababa Fine Arts School in 1957/58 is closely linked with another well known modernist painter and educator, Ale Felege Selam Heruy, a proud descendant of *Alaqa* (a learned priest) Heruy of Dima Giorgis (fig. 3). *Alaqa* Heruy was a traditional painter of the late nineteenth century known for his masterpieces at the churches of Entoto Mariam and Arada Giorgis (St. George) in Addis Ababa as well those in the town of Fitche. He is particularly remembered for his painting for the church of St. George of the 1986 Battle of Adwa.[11] His son, Emaelaf Heruy, Ale Felege Selam Heruy's uncle, is recognized for his numerous monumental murals

Fig. 2   Agegnehu Engida
Self Portrait, 1944
Oil on canvas
19 7/8 x 15 in.
(50.5 x 38.1 cm.)
Collection of the National
Museum of Ethiopia

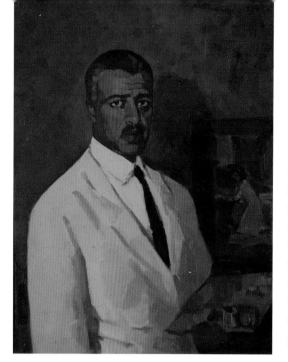

and portraits of Emperor Haile Selassie and other prominent personalities of his time. One could say that Ale Felege Selam Heruy inherited his artistic talent from these notable ancestors and himself made a great contribution to his country as a painter, founder of the modern fine arts school and educator.

Ato Ale, or Mister Ale, as his students call him, was born in 1924 and taught himself to draw and paint as a child. He graduated with distinction from Addis Ababa Technical School and was offered the opportunity by Emperor Haile Selassie to study mechanical engineering abroad. However, the artist recalls that the Minister of Education used the scholarship funds to send a member of his family abroad to study instead. Ale Felege found a job as a garage mechanic and secured boarding at a school, where he spent his leisure time drawing and painting portraits of the students, which were displayed in the dining hall. On a visit to the school to present gifts to the students, the Emperor admired the portraits and asked to meet the artist (figs. 4-5). Upon seeing Ale Felege again, he was surprised that he had not gone abroad to study and offered to provide another scholarship, this time to attend art school. After five years studying art education and fine arts, Ale Felege was awarded the BFA degree by the School of the Art Institute of Chicago. After a sixth year working to save money, he spent three months traveling in Europe before returning to Ethiopia in 1954.[12]

Ale Felege Selam Heruy came home with the aspiration of teaching and encouraging young Ethiopians. Although there was no art school to speak of, he began modestly by teaching students he recruited from high schools in Addis Ababa. His art classes were conducted in the old *Ras* Imiru

compound where he had rented a house. As he watched his students progress and thirst for more, he dreamed of developing a full-fledged program and building an art school. Hence, he organized a fundraising exhibition of works by his students and invited members of the royal family, diplomats from the various embassies and friends, enticing them to buy works of art for a good cause. Although the Emperor was unable to attend the exhibition, his son, Crown Prince Asfawossen, and Minister of Education and Fine Arts Kebede Mikael were present.

The show was successful and *Ato* Ale was able to raise 76,000 Ethiopian dollars, at the time equivalent to $38,000.[13] He presented a check for this amount to the Emperor, arguing the need for the creation of an art school and requesting the Emperor's help to make it happen. The Emperor, impressed by *Ato* Ale's determination, immediately authorized the release of funds and instructed Kebede Mikael to cooperate with the project. Thus, in 1957/58 under the supervision of Ale Felege Selam Heruy, Kebede Mikael and Ethiopian architect Mikael Teodros, the Addis Ababa Fine Arts School was established with Ale Felege Selam Heruy as its first director (fig. 6). The students whom *Ato* Ale was teaching at his Saturday and Sunday art classes and a few recruits from other parts of the country were the first to enroll.

The ribbon cutting ceremony was performed by Emperor Haile Selassie himself. As a patron of the arts, the Emperor was committed to the development and advancement of the fine arts. The following quote is from his opening address:

> Works of Art have existed in our country since time immemorial and their manifestation and development have been evidenced throughout history. Such evidences are witnessed on the walls of monasteries and churches and in the ruins of ancient palaces. Though many have succumbed to destruction by various wars, those that are still standing in places such as Lalibela, Gondar, Begemdir, Shoa, Gojjam and other areas are admired and praised by those who have seen them. These works of art attest to great achievements of the past. Therefore it is essential they are made available to the

inheritors of such creativity who would use them in a modern way. They are to be known to young Ethiopians who would follow in the footsteps of the past and find them to be a source of pride and inspiration.

We made the determination to insure that young and talented youth receive training about art of the past and create modern art that is inspired by it. It is important that tradition is referenced in a synthesis of new and modern ways. It is with such a synthesis in mind that the arts should develop and thus we give serious consideration to the field. Works of art created in such manner would show Ethiopia's aspiration toward the culture and spirit of world civilization and we hope that the results travel to foreign countries to bear witness for our efforts.

We are also equally committed toward efforts made in the development of music and creative writing. As artists, distance yourselves from the production of art works that are based on materialistic spirit and tendencies, for you don't expect flowers to bloom without planting them in a fertile soil. As you start your work avoid temptations from such trivialities.

We admire the work of the Creator not only for the things he provides us to nourish our bodies but also for the beauty that we observe around us. It is this aspect of creation that we can truly enjoy if we look and search beyond the material aspect of creativity.

We have repeatedly said that it is the completing of a task that is challenging, for it is easier to start the task. Hence, it is our wish to see the fruits of your labor in all their abundance and to let you know that we are pleased by what we have seen to date.[14]

The First Years of the Addis Ababa Fine Arts School

For the first group of students to enroll at the Addis Ababa Fine Arts School, Director Ale Felege Selam Heruy arranged that each receive a government-funded stipend of thirty Ethiopian birr a month. As time went on *Ato* Ale continued to solicit for assistance from the diplomatic corps and, through their cooperation, their respective governments began to donate materials and tools.[15] Hence, in the early days of the school there were ample materials and tools and their effective use was demonstrated by exceptional works produced by the students.

Securing faculty was initially a challenge. Because there had not previously been an art program capable of training art teachers, Ethiopian artists were not prepared to teach in an art school setting. *Ato* Ale went again to foreign embassies for assistance and also visited various secondary schools hoping to recruit teachers. While the latter effort was to no avail, a few enquiries did yield positive results from diplomatic circles. Notable among expatriate faculty in the 1950s and '60s were Herbert Seiler, an Austrian sculptor who taught anatomy, figure drawing and sculpture; Vincenzo Fumo, an Italian painter who had come to Ethiopia as a soldier of Mussolini and taught painting; Karl Heinz Hansen (also known as Hansen Bahia), a German graphic artist who taught printmaking; and Wendy Kindred, an American painter and retired professor of art from the University of Maine at Fort Kent who also taught printmaking.

At the time the only other Ethiopian teacher other than Ale Felege Selam Heruy was calligraphy teacher Yigazu Bisrat (1926-1979), who worked for the Ministry of Education and Fine Arts as an illustrator and was asked to transfer to the Fine Arts School. Yigazu had not studied art abroad, but was one of the few Ethiopian artists who apprenticed under the pioneers of modernism, Abebe Wolde Giorgis and Agegnehu Engida. Yigazu was fondly known to his students by the name "Irgibu" or "Dove" due to his gentle mannerisms (fig. 7).

top to bottom

Fig. 4 Ale Felege Selam Heruy
The Emperor with Children
1973, oil on canvas
51 x 67 in. (129.5 x 170 cm.)
Collection of the artist
This painting was commissioned by the head mistress of a school, pictured at right. Haile Selassie frequently visited schools to inspect students' work and distribute small gifts such as fruit or cakes.

Fig. 5 *The Emperor with Children* (detail)

Fig. 6 Studios and classrooms for the Addis Ababa Fine Arts School were housed in this building until new facilities were constructed in 1997. Photograph by Achamyeleh Debela

top to bottom

Fig. 7   Abayneh Dinku, secretary of the Addis Ababa Fine Arts School from 1965 to 1967 (left), with faculty members Yigazu Bisrat (center) and Vincenzo Fumo (right). Photograph courtesy of the Institute of Ethiopian Studies, Addis Ababa University

Fig. 8   Faculty of the Addis Ababa Fine Arts School in the 1960s at an exhibition of paintings by Gebre Kristos Desta, from left to right: Tadesse Belayneh, Bisrat Bekele, Tadesse Gizaw, Gebre Kristos Desta, Yigazu Bisrat, Abdurahman Sherif. Photograph courtesy of the Institute of Ethiopian Studies, Addis Ababa University

The founding of the Addis Ababa Fine Arts School ushered in a new era. Ethiopian artists trained abroad began to return home to practice their art as well as share it by teaching at the school and changing the faculty make-up (fig. 8). In 1962 Gebre Kristos Desta, an extraordinary young poet and painter, returned from Germany where he studied at the Werkschule fur Bildende Künste und Gestaltung, an art school in Cologne (fig. 9). In 1966 Skunder Boghossian, another brilliant painter, returned from France where he studied at the Ecole nationale supérior des beaux arts de Paris and the Académie de la Grande Chaumière (fig. 10). Ale Felege Selam Heruy recruited both artists and gave them faculty positions at the Fine Arts School. They infused a new creative energy into their students. Through their involvement with solo exhibitions as well as collaborative artistic activities, they gave birth to a new era, each in his own way. Encouraged by their teachers, students learned the fundamentals of art making and began to experiment. They held solo and group shows and soon attracted their own followings.[16]

The initial objectives of the Addis Ababa Fine Arts School were to train art instructors who would teach at the elementary and secondary levels and to produce professional artists who would either specialize in graphic design or become freelance painters and sculptors. While well-intentioned, the five-year course of study was actually geared more toward producing professional artists than teachers with a strong art education background.

Until the Marxist Derg regime began in 1974, a student at the Fine Arts School was required to take a five-year course of study leading to graduation with a diploma. The foundation years emphasized fundamentals of drawing, painting and sculpture. Watercolor and oil techniques; anatomy and figure drawing; landscape painting; and a few courses in the history of Western art were also included. These studies were focused on realistic rendering via observation. A fourth-year student could begin to experiment and pursue independent studies under the wings of a particular faculty member. This was particularly true of the final year when a student was expected to produce a major work, which usually took the form of an outdoor sculpture or mural, or, for those who chose graphics as their major, development of a portfolio. In addition to

art courses, other subjects such as English language and composition and psychology were offered when faculty was available.

The Addis Ababa Fine Arts School soon began to produce artists of the highest caliber who went on to study abroad. Some received scholarships before they finished their five-year program and left for eastern European countries as early as 1960 and 1961. A large number of graduates were trained in the Soviet Union and/or other Eastern Bloc countries such as Hungary, Yugoslavia and Poland. Some graduates joined the local workforce in various sectors of government and in private agencies. Others were employed by the public school system despite their lack of preparation in the area of art education, which limited their effectiveness as art teachers. Before the arrival of these art school graduates, the only art experience offered to most students in the public school system had been occasional handicraft projects, which were subsequently displayed at the annual parents' day.[17]

Despite the changing face of the faculty due to the return of Ethiopian artists, the curriculum stayed practically the same until the rise in 1974 of the Marxist Derg regime under Mengistu Haile Mariam. The school underwent a tremendous change during the seventeen years of this dictatorship. The curriculum and course of study were changed from five to four years, with the first two years dedicated to foundation courses and the third and fourth years to specialization. Emphasis was placed on subjects with greatest potential for use in political propaganda, such as graphics and mural painting.

Students worked under new pressures that led to nervous breakdowns for some, while others fled to live in exile. Faculty also worked in situations that are incomprehensible today, and the school became quite dilapidated. The Ministry of Culture and Sports was entrusted to construct a socialist culture in Ethiopia. This ministry proclaimed its objectives: "To arrange for the organization and promotion of culture and the arts in accordance with the principles of socialism and to encourage the creative power of the masses in the fine arts."[18] The ministry supervised music, painting, theater, cinema and literary creations. The development of Prop Art or slogan art was highly praised as an outcome of the glorious revolution. Fine Arts School students, along with some faculty members, were transported across the country and asked to paint large canvases with warm, vibrant colors to be hung in front of public buildings. When the works of students and faculty were deemed less than satisfactory, artists were brought from communist countries, notably North Korea, whose artists produced huge posters of people with Korean features in Ethiopian garb.

Modernist artists who enjoyed international acclaim were severely criticized in a UNESCO treatise by Alem Eshete. The author proclaimed: "Pre-revolutionary art exhibitions included works of high artistic quality, executed according to the latest international standard techniques. However, our famous artists of the past had little or no sense of 'artistic responsibility' to society. None of them played a role of edification or tried to improve the unjust conditions of the oppressed

masses." The text of the brochure states further that "realist or abstract, they all painted either for psychic gratification or for the local or international market. Ethiopian painting was an elitist art that aimed at the rich feudal-bourgeois magnates, diplomatic international circles, the wealthy tourists and in a few cases, the stock market of the advanced capitalist world."[19] Such verbiage epitomizes the kind of psychological attack aimed at leading artists whose works did not conform to revolutionary principles.

The Mengistu regime was overthrown in 1991, ushering in a period of greater freedom for the Fine Arts School. A positive development was its 1999/2000 merger with the Addis Ababa University as the School of Fine Arts and Design (figs. 11-12). Subsequently, aging and deteriorating offices, classrooms and galleries were renovated; new classroom facilities and a library were constructed; and resources such as computers and other office equipment were secured. Perhaps most significantly, an extensive revamping of the curriculum was undertaken to align the school with the academic standards and course offerings appropriate for a university department. The school now awards baccalaureate degrees rather than the previous diploma in fine arts.

In 1997 the Federal Democratic Republic of Ethiopia endorsed a new cultural policy intended to restructure the office in charge of cultural affairs to make its operation commensurate with a democratic system. The policy supports Article

top to bottom

Fig. 9   Gebre Kristos Desta working on a painting, date unknown. Photograph courtesy of the Institute of Ethiopian Studies, Addis Ababa University

Fig. 10   Skunder Boghossian (left) teaching a class at the Addis Ababa Fine Arts School in the late 1960s. Photograph by Achamyeleh Debela

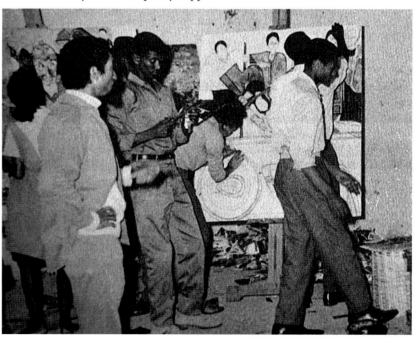

51/3 of the federal constitution of Ethiopia, which states that the government "shall establish and implement national standards and basic policy criteria for public health, education, science and technology as well as for the protection and preservation of cultural and historical legacies." Section 9 of the policy addresses "Spread of Cultural Knowledge," and includes the following items:

9.1 Cultural themes shall be included into the educational curricula with the aim of integrating education with culture and thereby to shape the youth with a sense of cultural identity;

9.2 Educational programs reflecting the various cultures of the country shall be transmitted by the mass media institutions in order to promote the cultural knowledge of the peoples of Ethiopia.[20]

Although the new policy acknowledges the importance of "cultural themes" in education, there is no specific mandate nor are there any guidelines in the policy for integrating the visual or performing arts into school curricula. A systematic and thorough needs assessment must be a prerequisite to implementation of a comprehensive art education curriculum based on what is culturally pertinent as well as practical for the school systems.

Furthermore, the national development policy of the party in control of the current government, the Ethiopian Peoples Revolutionary Democratic Front, is based on the ethnic origin and physical geographic location of Ethiopian peoples. Accordingly, its newly designed boundaries predicated on the above premise dictate educational policy. For example, if the new policy were to be fully implemented, the School of Fine Arts and Design could only serve designated residents of a particular region, namely, the city of Addis Ababa and the region of Shoa in which it is located. Given that there is only one such school in the country, it does not require scientific research to deduce the result of such a policy. The School of Fine Arts and Design has always opened its doors to talented and aspiring artists from all parts of Ethiopia, to members of all ethnic groups and all nationalities.

It is time for a new policy to be formed that addresses art education, art history and the integration of technology and modern practices in the arts and design curricula with special attention to the inclusion of all relevant traditional and living art forms both at the practical and theoretical levels. Equipped with new and improved curricula, a well-developed departmental structure, strong leadership and a determined faculty, the School of Fine Arts and Design has the potential to make a tremendous contribution to the education of future artists, art historians and art educators, and to the preservation and promotion of the visual arts in Ethiopia.

Fig. 11   One of the administrative and classroom buildings of the School of Fine Arts and Design, Addis Ababa University.
Photograph by Rebecca Martin Nagy, 2005

1   Bahru Zewde, *A History of Modern Ethiopia, 1855-1991*(Athens, Ohio: Ohio University Press, 1991), 108-109.
2   Teshome G. Wagaw, *The Development of Higher Education and Social Change: An Ethiopian Experience* (East
        Lansing: Michigan State University Press, 1990), 72.
3   U.S. Library of Congress. "Education During Imperial Rule." U.S. Library of Congress.
        http://www.countrystudies.us/ethiopia/70.htm.
4   Haile Selassie went into exile in Great Britain during the Italian Fascist occupation of 1936-1941.
5   In 1917, when the princess Zawditu, daughter of the late Emperor Menilek II, was crowned Empress of Ethiopia, her 25-
        year-old cousin, *Ras* Tafari Makonnen, was declared regent and heir to the throne. Eleven years later, in 1928, Zawditu
        elevated the crown prince to the position of *Negus* or king. With the death of Zawditu in 1930, *Negus* Tafari reached the
        pinnacle of the Ethiopian power structure as *Neguse Negest*, King of Kings or Emperor. The new Emperor adopted his
        baptismal name of Haile Selassie (Power of the Trinity).
6   Mengistu Lemma, "Modern Amharic Literature: The Task Ahead," *Voice of Ethiopia* (May 19, 1965): 2-4.
7   Taye Tadesse, *Short biographies of some Ethiopian artists, 1869-1957,* rev. ed. (Addis Ababa: Kuraz Publishing
        Agency, 1991), 16.
8   Although the government acknowledged the importance of art education, the first curriculum in art education was not
        developed until 2001 at the School of Fine Arts and Design of Addis Ababa University. Until additional faculty with
        appropriate qualifications and adequate resources can be secured, the curriculum cannot be fully implemented.
9   After the founding of the Addis Ababa Fine Arts School in 1957/58, students at the school often interacted with the
        traditional painters employed by the Ministry of Education and Fine Arts. In the absence of a curriculum in the history of
        Ethiopian art, these conversations provided students an opportunity to learn something of the artistic traditions of their
        country. Prominent folk artists employed by the Ministry included Mezmur Zedawit and his brother Araya Zedawit, Imailaf
        Hiruyi, Aleqa Gabre Sellassie Adil, Wolda Medhin Yirugassu, Alemayehou Afework, Sahla Dingl Wolde Tsadik, Atnaf Seged
        Desta, Aleka Gabra Mariam Wagayou, Belachew Yimar, Yemane Brhan Tembal and Mamre Desta Birke.
10 Taye Tadesse, *Short biographies of some Ethiopian artists, 1869-1957,* rev. ed. (Addis Ababa: Kuraz Publishing
        Agency, 1991), 83.
11 This work so angered the Italian Fascists that they burned the church. After the end of the Ethio-Italian war, the church
        was rebuilt and new murals were commissioned from Emaelaf Heruy and Afewerk Tekle.
12 Personal conversation with the artist, June 2005.
13 The Ethiopian dollar was used until 1976, when it was replaced by the Ethiopian birr.
14 Translated by Achamyeleh Debela from the Amharic language twenty-fifth anniversary victory day commemoration
        publication (Addis Ababa: Ministry of Information and Tourism, 1958).
15 Canvases, brushes, oil colors and art books were donated by the Soviet Union two years after the opening of the school.
        Four years later Germany donated oil colors, pastels and a silk screen printing press. The Polish government donated a
        movie camera. These and other donations supplemented the meager budget provided to the young art school by the
        Ministry of Education and Fine Arts. The Ministry, to its credit, paid the salaries of administrators, faculty and staff, and
        continues to do so. Eshetu Tiruneh, unpublished Amharic manuscript on the history of the Addis Ababa Fine Arts School,
        Modern Art in Ethiopia and the Development of the Fine Arts School of Addis Ababa, 1872–1991 (2000).
16 Skunder's notable students included Zerihun Yetmgeta, Wosene Kosrof, Tesfaye Tessema, Alemayehu Gebra Medhin
        and Girmey Hiwet, to name a few. Gebre Kristos' successful students included Yohannes Gedamu, Achamyeleh Debela,
        Berhe Temelso and Desta Hagos, to name a few.
17 Previous to the placement of art school graduates in the public school system, students received their exposure to art by way
        of history or sociology studies through handicraft projects such as wood carving or covering wine bottles with woven jute.
        Their work was subsequently displayed at the school's annual parents' day.
18 Seyoum Wolde, "Some aspects of post-revolution visual arts in Ethiopia," *Proceedings of the Ninth International Conference on
        Ethiopian Studies, Moscow, August 26-29, 1986* (Moscow: Nauka Publishers, Central Department of Oriental Literature,
        1988): 7-25.
19 Alem Eshete, *The Cultural Situation in Socialist Ethiopia* (Paris: United Nations Educational, Scientific and Cultural
        Organization, 1982), 27-28.
20 Embassy of The Federal Democratic Republic of Ethiopia. "The Federal Democratic Republic of Ethiopia Cultural Policy."
        Embassy of The Federal Democratic Republic of Ethiopia. http://www.ethioembassy.org.uk/fact%20file/a-z/culture.htm

Fig. 12   Sculpture on the grounds
          of the School of Fine Arts
          and Design, Addis Ababa
          University. Photograph by
          Achamyeleh Debela, 2006

Florescence of the Arts in the "New Flower" (Addis Ababa) before 1974

Heran Sereke-Brhan and Shiferaw Bekele

Heran Sereke-Brhan is academic director of the School for International Training's Study Abroad Program in Ethiopia and is affiliated with the Institute of Ethiopian Studies of Addis Ababa University. She received her doctorate in African history at Michigan State University. She worked as curatorial assistant and education specialist for the 2003 exhibition *Ethiopian Passages: Contemporary Art from the Diaspora* at the National Museum of African Art, Smithsonian Institution. Her research interests include the recent history of the visual and performing arts in Ethiopia. In 2006 she edited *Gebre Kristos Desta, Expansive Pathway . . . Lifetime Traveler: An Anthology of Poetry* and rendered many of the Amharic poems in English.

Shiferaw Bekele is associate professor in the department of history at Addis Ababa University, where he also received undergraduate and graduate degrees in history. He has published articles on the political and social history of Ethiopia from the eighteenth to the twentieth centuries in numerous scholarly journals and edited *Economic History of Ethiopia: The Imperial Era 1941-74* (1995). In 2004, he served as guest editor and contributing author for the *Journal of Ethiopian Studies Special Issue: Tribute to Gebre Kristos Desta and Skunder Boghossian.*

Addis Ababa of the 1960s was a city of intense artistic activity and creative explosion. Performance, literary and visual artists were prolific, producing high quality works that garnered national and international attention. Most were keenly engaged in following developments in the rest of Africa and in the West. Their favorite subjects of discussion included debates on the nature of art and its place in developing countries like Ethiopia. Public discourse on the complex offerings and drawbacks of modernization found their way into the arts as poets, authors, playwrights and musicians grappled with issues of identity in a transforming world. Critics, commentators and scholars have variably characterized these "golden years" of contemporary Ethiopian art as a period of "renaissance," as the flowering of an "Addis Spring" and a vibrant "florescence" of creativity.

Perhaps one starting point for the history of contemporary art is the liberation of the country from Italian rule in 1941. The following decades witnessed the slow process of re-establishing legitimacy and consolidating political power. The task at hand was no longer territorial expansion nor the absorption and annexation of kingdoms, but the more elusive challenge of crafting nation from empire and building a modernizing state. Upon his return from exile in 1941, Emperor Haile Selassie resumed with great gusto initiatives that had begun before the Italian invasion. Ironically, the Italian occupation had unwittingly facilitated part of the new transformation by almost completely destroying provincial levies and removing the local power base of regional nobility. Unlike colonial institutions elsewhere in Africa though, Fascist administrative structures were dismantled by the Italians before the arrival of the liberation army into Addis Ababa, such that rebuilding had to begin from nothing.

Modernization of state institutions in the form of bureaucratization was given top priority. For the first time, the newly reconstructed state included a centralized national army complete with ground, air and naval forces. Haile Selassie created an immense civilian administrative framework and government employees at all levels were paid salaries for the first time. Through these and other changes, the Emperor sought to propel the nation forward on what he believed to be the path of progress and enlightenment.

Education was the Emperor's chosen vehicle for modernization. The Emperor's commitment to this cause indicated its critical role in restoration. The new work force that entered civil service drew from an educated elite. The Emperor was credited for creating this group by keenly following the personal development of many and actively cultivating their loyalty. This astute arrangement initially provided Haile Selassie with an alternative support base with which to balance conservative tendencies in government.

The challenge of expanding educational facilities was exacerbated by the fact that schools had been closed, destroyed and looted during the liberation struggle. There were practically no teachers, appropriate buildings or materials to launch the daunting task. Emergency measures were undertaken to jump start the system. Thus young boys and girls were moved through primary school with unprecedented speed and were ready for their London Matriculation Examination as early as 1943 when the first secondary school (Kotebe) opened.[1] In 1946 the government opened the second secondary school, General Wingate School, and in the same year upgraded the Tafari Makonnen School to offer secondary education. To address the demand for teachers, a training school was established in 1944.[2] Nine years after Liberation, the state was able to found a tertiary institution of learning, the University College of Addis Ababa, which began offering courses in December 1950.[3] Enrollment in the state education system (primary, secondary and tertiary) grew from 20,000 in 1944 to 820,436 in 1973.[4]

Modern Education and the Arts

Students received first-class education in these newly established schools. All were in Addis Ababa and represented the best of what the country had to offer. The published curriculum of elementary education gave considerable attention to art education.[5] It was designed to introduce pupils to three principal branches of the arts—painting, sculpture and architecture.[6] Children would be taught rudimentary painting and sculpting. Creators of the curriculum believed that "the pleasure of working with colored pigments and with materials having intrinsic color attraction is a most valued element in the emotional experience of children." As they moved on to the fifth class, pupils would be taught appreciation of art through exposure to "the best accomplishment in art of painting, sculpture and architecture."[7] Students were to see and discuss masterpieces of painting and sculpture. National heritage was not to be overlooked either. "Whenever available," the curriculum states, "Ethiopian paintings should be used for picture study."[8] Art appreciation was to be reinforced by music education, intended to develop in the pupil "a taste for music."[9] Like art

education, music would be taught over six years of elementary education.

Students were to be exposed to classical literature—poetry, plays and novels—as they moved on to secondary levels. The teaching curricula of the newly established secondary schools would include sizeable portions of Western literature and creative writing. Literature was considered an important component of learning English language, so that stage by stage, students would be exposed to the leading world classics. For instance, the curriculum for grade 10 stipulates, "novels and short stories should be read. Poetry and possibly 'Caesar' or 'Macbeth' may be enjoyed by any advanced class."[10] Students read and studied Shakespeare's major tragedies and comedies in elite schools like Wingate, Kotebe and Tafari Makonnen. The curriculum also emphasized the importance of writing. For instance, for grade 11 students "as much out-of-class reading as possible should be encouraged, to strengthen vocabulary and command of English…students should be able to recognize personification, exaggeration, understated puns and onomatopoeia."[11] They practiced their writing skills until they progressed to experimenting with creative compositions.

Most students at these elite schools were encouraged to be avid readers, a habit that later broadened their artistic quest and emboldened their explorations. Across schools, similar curricula in literature served as a window to the outside world and presented some sort of uniformity of worldviews, evident when the generation later came of age. Chances are high that painter/poet Gebre Kristos Desta first encountered English Romantic poetry or poet/playwright Tsegaye Gebre-Medhin discovered Shakespeare in these school settings. Because education and the arts were so linked, it may not have been a coincidence that the Menilek School was the place that early theater actors got their first training under the tutorship of Belete Gebre. Menilek was also the first home of the Fine Arts School until part of its land was used to put up the permanent building where the school still stands.[12]

Upon completing their secondary education, students sat for the London Matriculation Examination and many passed—a sure testimony

of the standard of their training. In the late 1940s most of them were sent for higher studies on government scholarships to Europe, the United States and Canada. After 1950, those who completed their secondary education first attended the University College of Addis Ababa before going abroad for further studies.

Not surprisingly, many of the important actors in the florescence of the arts in the 1960s were products of this educational system. The newly established schools were meeting places for young students of various backgrounds and class affiliations. Attending boarding school in the increasingly cosmopolitan capital often meant separation from immediate family and surroundings. Classmates of diverse origins came to substitute for family and the bustling urban center became home away from home for many.

Although they would not have been aware of their calling at the time, schoolmates from Tafari Makonnen and General Wingate schools would come to dominate the art scene of the 1960s. Among those who attended these secondary schools were poet/art critic Solomon Deressa, painter/poet Gebre Kristos Desta, authors Sebhat Gebre-Egziabher and Sahle Selassie Berhane-Mariam along with poet/playwright Tsegaye Gebre-Medhin and author/dramatist Tesfaye Gessese. The state often saw to it that students were sent to elite institutions in Europe and the United States to continue their studies. Playwright and author Mengistu Lemma and artist Afewerk Tekle were among the early group sent to England in 1947 to attend the London School of Economics and the Slade School of Fine Art, respectively. Later, Sebhat, Sahle Selassie and Solomon studied for their first degrees at the new University College in Addis Ababa and then went first to France then to the United States. Gebre Kristos went to Germany after a stint at the University College.

Whereas elsewhere in Africa, leaders like Kwame Nkrumah and Leopold Senghor employed the arts to express indignation against colonial rule and to affirm pride in national identity, Emperor Haile Selassie saw the arts as an important instrument in efforts to modernize Ethiopia. He encountered future painters and writers early in their careers as students staging or exhibiting works. The Emperor attended such events, regularly stopping

to encourage young artists and to note their accomplishments (fig. 1). He often saw to it that those who showed potential talent were trained in one or another branch of the arts. For instance, Tesfaye Gessese's ambition was to pursue law after completing his studies in the University College. The Emperor advised him to study theater instead and arranged for his scholarship in the United States. Ale Felege Selam Heruy, a man of no mean importance in the history of modern arts in Ethiopia, may not have chosen that path had the Emperor not noticed his talents as a young man and later sent him to a prestigious school in Chicago to study art education and painting. Haile Selassie was also personally involved in sending Skunder Boghossian to London, then Paris, to further his studies. The Emperor's patronage of the arts was both symbolic and practical. He identified in personal and public ways as ultimate architect of modern education, a man who embodied the image of a culturally aware progressive.

Institutions of Art (1950s-1960s)

Emperor Haile Selassie was also actively involved in building cultural institutions. He placed education and the arts together under the Ministry of Education and Fine Arts, which he headed for many years. He set up a Department of Fine Arts in the Ministry and Abebe Wolde Giorgis, a sculptor whom he had sent to France for training before the war, was made its head. His assistant was Agegnehu Engida, another artist with similar background.

Following his return from the United States in 1954, Ale Felege Selam Heruy worked to establish the Addis Ababa Fine Arts School and was made its director, a position he held until the revolution of 1974. Afewerk Tekle returned from his studies and European tour in 1955 and was given several commissions that established his reputation and provided him with sufficient income to build his own spacious studio.

Institutions for theater and music were also established soon after the restoration of the country's independence. The Addis Ababa Municipality created a department of theater, music and painting. A musical troupe was established under the guidance of two Armenian men from the Nalbandian family. They trained a group in modern music, arranging pieces for big

Fig. 1   Emperor Haile Selassie with Gebre Kristos Desta at the opening of the artist's exhibition in 1963. Photograph courtesy of the Institute of Ethiopian Studies, Addis Ababa University

band performances using European instruments. Their performances took place in the hall provided by the Municipality, the same hall used to stage plays and host art exhibitions.

Established in 1934 to generate patriotic propaganda, the *Hager Fikir Mahber* (literally Love of Country Association) was active until the imminent advent of Italian invaders into Addis in 1936. Its founding father, Mekonnen Habte Wold, revived it in 1942 and continued to guide it until his death in 1960. The Emperor closely followed its activities. Mekonnen aimed to build the *Mahber* into a cultural institution that would draw upon performance arts to build unity, nationalism and patriotism, as well as to promote loyalty to the government and its ruler. In 1942 Mekonnen recruited Beshah Tekle Mariam who assembled a musical troupe that was quickly trained to offer its first public musical performance in February of the same year.

In 1946 the government called upon the musical troupe to transmit songs on the national radio. About the same time *Hager Fikir* also organized national tours for its performers. They traveled by bus, truck and sometimes on foot and horseback. The *Hager Fikir Mahber* together with the Addis Ababa Municipality's Music and Drama Department thus began to diffuse modern music, theater and presentation throughout the country. The Grand Silver Jubilee celebration of Haile Selassie's coronation in 1955 led to the renovation and expansion of its hall, enabling it to have a much larger audience. In 1960 its long-time director was killed in an abortive coup d'etat. Finally in 1967/8

its name was slightly modified to *Hager Fikir Theater*.

The coronation celebration was occasion for cultural renewal. The Emperor recognized the need to have an additional venue with a professionally equipped stage, lighting and sound system and supported the Municipality's efforts to convert an unfinished Italian building for this purpose. With the fast-approaching date of the coronation, construction was completed swiftly in one year. A statue of a large lion and a fountain symbolizing the plume of the Emperor's hat and the arc of his entourage's swords graced the plaza at the side of the building (fig. 2).[13] Emperor Haile Selassie inaugurated the new facility, Haile Selassie I Theater, on November 10, 1955, and attended the first musical performance there a week later (fig. 3).

Haile Selassie I University established its Creative Arts Center in 1963. The Center very quickly began hosting leading literary, visual and performance artists such as Afewerk Tekle, Gebre Kristos Desta, Skunder Boghossian, Tsegaye Gebre-Medhin, Mengistu Lemma, Ashenafi Kebede and Solomon Deressa. Tsefaye Gessese was its first deputy director and later its director. Student volunteers were recruited to act in famous experimental plays such as Samuel Beckett's *Waiting for Godot*, Edward Albee's *The Zoo Story*, and his *Who's Afraid of Virginia Woolf*, as well as to participate in works by upcoming Ethiopian playwrights. Kebede Mikael's translation of *Romeo and Juliet* and Mengistu's *Alača Gabča* (Unequal Marriage) were staged. Tsegaye's *Tewodros* was

left to right

Fig. 2   The stone lion sculpture created by French sculptor Maurice Calka for the plaza adjacent to the Haile Selassie I Theater (now the National Theater) inaugurated in 1955. Photograph by Rebecca Martin Nagy, 2006

Fig. 3   Telela Kebede and Tadele Tamrat as lovers in a performance of Hugo von Hofmannsthal's 1912 morality play *Jedermann (Everyman)*. The play was translated into Amharic by Hailu Desta in 1959/60 to be performed for the imperial court at the Haile Selassie I Theater. Photograph courtesy of Getachaw Debalke

attended by the Emperor (fig. 4). The Center also provided space for art exhibitions, and works by Afewerk Tekle, Ale Felege Selam Heruy, Gebre Kristos Desta, Skunder Boghossian and Zerihun Yetmgeta were displayed. Tesfaye Lemma led the Center's house band, the Ethiopia Orchestra. The band experimented with traditional instruments and musical arrangements, developing a signature sound. The Creative Arts Center rapidly became the hub of contemporary Ethiopian arts. Unfortunately its activities were not sustained. It ceased to function, for all practical purposes, by the end of the 1960s, due mainly to the fact that the university administration did not provide sufficient funds for its operation.

The Haile Selassie I Prize Trust, also established in 1963, was the other institution that promoted the growth of the arts and literature. The Trust

left to right

Fig. 4   Desta Hagos' painting *The Stage* (1969) captures the energy and creativity of the theater in Addis Ababa in the 1960s.
Oil and collage on board
33 x 42 7/8 in. (83.8 x 108.9 cm)
Collection of Desta Hagos

Fig. 5   Gebre Kristos Desta receiving the Haile Selassie I Prize Trust Award from Emperor Haile Selassie and Prime Minister Aklilu Habtewold in 1965. Photograph courtesy of the Institute of Ethiopian Studies, Addis Ababa University

was set up to encourage an array of achievements by giving awards in literature; the arts (painting and sculpture); research in Ethiopian studies; teaching; welfare and philanthropy; and business, agriculture and industry. In its ten-year life span (1963-1973), it awarded the prize to Afewerk Tekle, Gebre Kristos Desta and Skunder Boghossian for their accomplishments in painting, and to Kebede Mikael, Tsegaye Gebre-Medhin, Mengistu Lemma, Haddis Alemayehu and *Blatten Geta* Mahteme Selassie Wolde-Mesqel in literature (fig. 5). The selection procedure was rigorous, which explains

why only three painters and five creative writers were given the award in ten years. The prize acquired a prestigious reputation in the society and inspired artists to perfect their craft.

Initially established in 1944/ 1945 by the Ministry of Education, the music school functioned with a small budgetary allocation and was neglected for years. It did not have an appropriate building, nor was it fully equipped with the necessary facilities. The curriculum lacked direction and there were no regular students. Its expatriate teaching staff trained students in European music, with particular focus on the classical genre. As demands for a proper music school grew, the government began to take serious measures. Ashenafi Kebede, an Ethiopian trained in ethnomusicology in the United States, was appointed principal of the school and its budgetary allocation was raised.[14] The school also obtained external assistance.

Ashenafi began reorganizing the school in 1966. Regular students were admitted and a new curriculum, which included studying Ethiopian music and traditional instruments, was designed. The schools objectives were defined more precisely. Among its aims was to train teachers for the school system and to educate people who could "develop and enrich the music world of Ethiopia."[15] Five teaching departments were initiated for those who wanted to study violin, piano, instrumental music, musical education and Ethiopian music. A slow Ethiopianization process of the teaching staff took place, and Ashenafi secured the funds to erect a fully equipped building. In honor of the fourth century Ethiopian saint credited for annotating church liturgy, Ashenafi renamed the National Music School as the Yared Music School in July 1970.[16]

Performance Arts and Programs

In the late 1950s and early 1960s, plays staged in Addis Ababa were mostly religious and moralizing in content, with titles like *David and Orion*, *Hannibal* and *Crucifixion* (fig. 6). The role of theater was primarily to convey didactic teachings of the Bible, much like the leanings of early painters toward religious themes in their works. Early writers such as Kebede Mikael, Mekonnen Indalkachew and Deressa Amente adopted the same teaching tone in their works. With the incident of the Italian invasion still fresh in public memory, patriotic plays such as *Afajeshign* (I am fighting for you) and *Almotkum Biye Alwashim* (I won't pretend I have not perished) conveyed values of courage and selfless sacrifice for the motherland.[17] Much would change in the 1960s with the appearance of works by Mengistu Lemma, Tsegaye Gebre-Medhin and Tesfaye Gessese, whose focus broadened to social issues and inequalities, thus placing human frailties more squarely at the forefront.

Beginning in 1959, the Haile Selassie I Theater also hosted highly anticipated annual music festivals to mark the New Year, simultaneously introducing new albums and musical talent to the public. As only a few could get seats in the crowded theater, most relied on the radio broadcast to follow the performances and herald the coming year. The festival was occasion to show off the accomplishments of big bands, notably the Imperial Body Guards, Army and Police Bands, most of whom had rehearsed in secret to outdo one another on this day. In this fiercely competitive ambience, the Imperial Body Guards often took the honors.

Big bands were prominent features of the cultural landscape of Addis Ababa in the 1960s. Each had its own areas of excellence. The Imperial Body Guards were at the forefront of jazz music, introducing a great number of enduring classics. Their repertoire was hailed as among the best in Africa.[18] Sahle Degago was a leading figure in popularizing the

music by penning compositions for vocalists and bands. The Police Band's string orchestra excelled in classical European music and trained its own violinists, cellists and conductors. Ethiopia's first academically trained composers, Ashenafi Kebede and Tsegaye Debalqe, emerged at this time (fig. 7). Ashenafi's work, *The Shepherd Flutist*, and Tsegaye's composition, *Gofere Hugnilegn* (Be My *Gofere*), garnered much admiration.[19] Both the Army and Police bands also performed popular music. The Police Band was famous for their rock 'n' roll music that borrowed stylistically from its western counterpart but substituted cultural content with Amharic lyrics. The house band of the National Theater acquired a reputation for its cabaret music with Getu Ayele as its most well-known vocalist.[20]

There were individual initiatives to record and document the flourishing musical scene for posterity. In 1948 the Emperor had given the *Hager Fikir Mahber* monopoly of importing and producing records. In 1969 Amaha Eshete broke this privilege by successfully producing his own records. He distributed his labels, venturing into an area previously handled by foreign businessmen. Amaha's effort gained him a sizeable clientele. His popularly frequented music shop named *Harambe* reflected the growing pan-African sentiment in the Addis of the late 1960s. Amaha also organized a private band (perhaps the first of its kind) named Soul Echoes. Philips-Ethiopia and Kiafa Records soon followed in his footsteps, producing more Ethiopian recordings.

Florescence—New Directions in the Arts

Political tensions that unsparingly revealed the fault-lines of the aging imperial leadership culminated in the watershed event of the 1960s, the attempted coup led by General Mengistu Neway. The coup coincided with the coming of age of Ethiopian artists and intellectuals who had attained formal education at home and abroad. It was in the early years of this decade that those who had studied theater, music, painting and literature in Europe and the United States returned home. Not surprisingly, many were variously influenced by their travels and studies abroad. In addition to those who strengthened friendships established earlier in secondary school and the University College, others had opportunities to meet and exchange thoughts and viewpoints while abroad.

Fig. 6 A production in 1955/56 of the religious play *David and Orion* by Ras Bitwoded at the Haile Selassie I Theater (now the National Theater). Photograph courtesy of Getachaw Debalke

In his recent article reminiscing about his friendship with Gebre Kristos Desta and Skunder Boghossian, author and critic Asfaw Damte recalls his meeting with these pioneers of contemporary Ethiopian art in Cologne (1960) and in Paris (1961), respectively.[21] He notes with some surprise that his first personal encounters with artist Afewerk Tekle and poet/playwright Tsegaye Gebre-Medhin also took place around the same time—not in Addis Ababa, but in London. Asfaw recollects the broader setting in which these meetings often took place. Ethiopian students in Britain, France and Germany had formed associations such as the Ethiopian Students Society in Great Britain and the umbrella organization, the Ethiopian Students Union in Europe. Such associations organized periodic conferences, which assembled an array of young, avid Ethiopians for an intense exchange of views on the political, social, economic and artistic changes taking place locally and globally. Interestingly, Asfaw notes that the imperial government underwrote some of the costs related to organizing these gatherings, in accordance, it seems, with the Emperor's interest in supporting modern education.[22]

Asfaw's description of his first meeting with Gebre Kristos reveals both the personal charisma of the gifted painter and poet and the high caliber of shared intellectual versatility and cultural fluency enjoyed by this generation of educated Ethiopians. A chance encounter at a café in Cologne blossomed into a discussion of philosophy that included the writings of Locke, Hume and Kant as well as a fiery debate on the tenets of empiricism versus scholasticism. The fact that Gebre Kristos was a painter did not register clearly in Asfaw's mind. Rather, his fit physique and mental agility remained a lasting first impression marking the beginning of years of friendship.

Europe was the setting for other formative encounters. Poet Laureate Tsegaye Gebre-Medhin shared his memories at a 2003 event honoring his life and works at the National Museum of African Art (Smithsonian) in Washington, D.C., He spoke of his days as a young man invited to study French experimental theater at the Comédie-Française under the mentorship of Louis Mignon in Paris. Although he knew of painter Skunder Boghossian, they did not meet until 1960 when he was invited to read poetry to a group of Ethiopian students in the Latin Quarter. They discussed their lives and Ethiopian arts over French wine. Five years later, they met again in the Latin Quarter and Tsegaye urged Skunder to send his works to the national committee selecting pieces for the First World Black Arts Festival in Dakar, Senegal.[23]

As the era of independence struggles unfolded on the continent, Ethiopian students and artists in London and Paris were deeply influenced by pan-African cultural consciousness and anti-colonial sentiments of their times. They were inspired by the writings of such luminaries as Cheikh Anta Diop and Leopold Senghor, whom some met in person. Paris of the 1960s was a vibrant center of African and African American creativity. Authors such as James Baldwin and Chester Himes came into contact with young Ethiopian writers, and the sounds of jazz musicians emanated from clubs and street corners of the city. Mengistu Lemma, Gebre Kristos Desta, Solomon Deressa and Tsegaye Gebre-Medhin would later pen creative writings that identified with the dislocation of racism, honored the struggles against colonialism, and observed the angst of confrontations with modernization.

Conversations that began abroad were quite often resumed in Addis Ababa. While the obvious reason for this continuity was the physical return home of key personalities in the arts, beneath it lay a matrix of friendships, shared educational experiences and world views, as well as the sustained, dynamic exchange of ideas that informed and enriched artistic explorations. Not long after their return, poets, writers, critics, painters and musicians of growing repute organized informal forums that met weekly or monthly in their homes, or later at the Creative Arts Center, to share works in progress. Asfaw Damte initiated one such group that included Mengistu Lemma, Tsegaye Gebre-Medhin, Tesfaye Gesesse, musicians and composers Ashenafi Kebede and Tsegaye Debalqe as well as Gebre Kristos Desta.[24]

Asfaw Damte indicates that the group met every Friday and assigned one member the task of presenting his own creation, or bringing works of interest to share and to discuss. Other artists were sometimes invited to present and join in conversations. Topics chosen included current theatrical productions, new exhibitions or musical concerts staged at the time in city. Notwithstanding differences in personality and approach, animated debates and strongly voiced opinions were shared in this gathering. As though they allowed themselves a different sort of vulnerability within the group, Asfaw records with undisguised affection his impressions of poetry readings by Mengistu Lemma and Gebre Kristos Desta. The opportunity of hearing pieces read by the authors themselves revealed a glimpse of inner inspiration and another level of craftsmanship not readily apparent by just reading the works. Some combination of youth and daring may have helped create the uninhibited nature of such exchanges.

As part of another group that included Solomon Deressa and Sebhat Gebre-Egziabher, Tesfaye Gessese also notes the freedom enjoyed between colleagues who did not shy away from stating honest opinions about the quality of each other's work.[25] Sometime in 1965, the Association for the Development of Ethiopian Music and Theater was established and Tsegaye Debalqe elected its first president. In the late 1960s Skunder Boghossian initiated the "Young Artists Group" to encourage students of the Fine Arts School to share experiences and organize exhibitions.

Although the groups were in many cases short-lived, their very existence announced a different approach to contemporary art. As both critics and creators, these playwrights, dramatists, painters and poets were attempting to map their own discourse with its internally governing sets of rules and balances. While some figures like Mengistu Lemma and Tsegaye Gebre-Medhin identified more closely with innovating language from within while exploring new themes in their works, others like Solomon Deressa and Gebre Kristos Desta were open to experimenting with possibilities, changing the stylistic appearance of poems and including imagery in their writings. Though their personalities were powerful individually and their works were defined boldly from the start, most of these artists of different temperament and leanings continued to confer with one another. The familiarity of their friendships, the intimacy of the settings and a deep appreciation of shared aesthetics and instinctive radicalism no doubt

provided intellectual stimulus and professional support to a quickly self-articulating group of observant and seemingly fearless men who crossed hitherto demarcated boundaries in their works.

Members of this loosely knit community of creativity supported one another in other ways as well. Writers and theater actors regularly attended exhibitions, while musicians and painters were present at theater performances, thus were constantly informed and inspired by one another's creativity. Asfaw Damte notes that Tsegaye Gebre-Medhin penned a poem evoking the intellectual quest of a poor student of *qene* (classical Amharic poetry), while listening to Gebre Kristos Desta read his piece "*YeBahir Qirdedoch*" (Sea Waves). He notes how author Sahle Selassie wrote of the vivid impression of Gebre Kristos' first exhibition. Thirty years later, Sahle Selassie was still haunted by the image of *Gypsy Girl*, Gebre Kristos' painting of a mysterious woman with reflective eyes.[26]

These internal dialogues were not exclusive. Haile Selassie's coronation celebrations in 1955 coincided with the launching of a new monthly magazine *Menen*, the express intent of which was to serve ladies and young women. Its columns were not limited to issues of beauty, fashion and women's health, but often featured columns on art and culture. Solomon Deressa and Sebhat Gebre-Egziabher regularly wrote about the arts in city newspapers and magazines such as *Addis Reporter*, *Menen* and *Ethiopian Mirror*, sharing their views on art happenings with the public. These publications contained reviews of plays and books as well as interviews with artists and theater

Fig. 7   The composer Ashenafi Kebede. Photograph courtesy of Getachaw Debalke

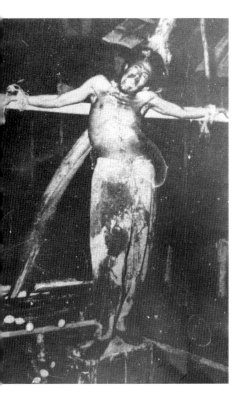

actors. Audience members wrote in their responses, actively engaging in the debate. Sebhat's witty columns still appear in newspapers periodically while Asfaw Damte continues to write prolifically about the state of Amharic literature. Because of their particular placement and perspective, pieces written by these writers now serve as among the most insightful sources on the cultural history of the period.

Artists of the florescence of the 1960s collaborated on projects beyond this public service. Besides his personal generosity, which compelled him to give his paintings and poetry away, Gebre Kristos Desta was an active example of one who would help colleagues in visually interpreting their works. He offered his free services to paint the backdrops for two of Tsegaye Gebre-Mesfin's plays, *Ha-Hu BeSidist Wur* (ABC in Six Months) and *Oda Oak Oracle* (fig. 8). Mulatu Astatke, the then up-and-coming gifted musician and composer who had begun experimenting with Ethiopian melodies and jazz arrangements, wrote musical accompaniments to Tsegaye's 1966 play *Yekermo Sew* (The Seasoned). Although closer in profession, the dynamic partnership of director Abate Mekuria and playwright Tsegaye resulted in epic productions with stage arrangements and superb acting that remains recorded as classics in public memory.

Innovation and Experimentation

A breakthrough in Ethiopian theater came with the staging of Tsegaye Gebre-Medhin's plays in Haile Selassie I Theater beginning in 1961. These plays were performed on a fully equipped stage, which made ample use of modern technology. Unlike previous plays, Tsegaye's centered on social themes. Inequalities of class and privilege were explored and struggles of the poor were depicted. Mengistu Lemma staged his comedies around the same time, imbuing his writing with discerning social commentary. In 1966 Tsegaye delved deeper into the psyche of the have-nots, portraying the ills of modernization and the chasm between generations in his acclaimed play *Yekermo Sew* (The Seasoned). This piece hinted at the playwright's affinity to the writings of famed British dramatist, Harold Pinter. The critics were full of praise.

In this same year, Skunder Boghossian launched his first exhibition in Addis after years of living in

London and Paris. He came back an accomplished painter who made concerted effort to draw on the motifs of traditional Ethiopian painting for inspiration. The public quickly bought his works. In the same year, Gebre Kristos Desta put up his second exhibition. His first exhibition (1963), soon after his return from training in Germany, had been a grand success. Both exhibitions offered the public a rich collection of abstract and semi-abstract paintings, which broke away from the mold by charting a new visual direction. As both Skunder and Gebre Kristos were instructors at the Addis Ababa Fine Arts School, they were able to teach and influence a generation of young artists, many of whom enjoy national and international recognition today.

In 1966 Haddis Alemayehu published his best-selling novel, *Fiker Eske Meqabir* (Love unto Death). The work was a departure from prevailing traditions, which began with the appearance of the first novel *Tobia* by Afework Gebre Yesus in 1908. The characters in *Fiker Eske Meqabir* were recognizable and plausible and the plot was well constructed. The magnificent prose narrates the story of a family set in the foreground of a changing Ethiopian society of the 1920s, a society that was encountering its first confrontations with the complex challenges of modernization. Readers and critics applauded the work as a major literary achievement. It continues to occupy its place as a classic of Ethiopian literature.

Other successful works shared the limelight. Berhanu Zerihun published perhaps his best novel, *Ye-Tewodros Enba* (The Tears of Tewodros), about the same time. It was a powerful criticism of the political and social establishment of the time through the allegory of Emperor Tewodros (reigned 1855-1868) and his struggle against the nobility and the church. With poetic prose, the author skillfully conveys power relationships between characters, lending insight into the dangers of idealist visions in conservative settings.

Tsegaye Gebre-Medhin, Sahle Selassie Berhane-Mariam, Dagnachew Worku and to a lesser extent Solomon Deressa wrote successful creative works in English. The first three writers published with Heinemann's prestigious *African Writers Series* where luminary African literary figures such as Chinua Achebe, Ngugi wa Thiong'o and Wole

Fig. 8 Wegayehu Negatu in a performance of Tsegaye Gebre Medhin's play *Ha-Hu BeSidist Wur (ABC in Six Months)* directed by Abate Mekuria at the Haile Selassie I Theater. Photograph courtesy of Getachaw Debalke

Soyinka, among others, published their major works in the 1960s and 1970s. By so doing, Ethiopian writers joined the pan-African literary movement of the period. Mengistu Lemma translated his play, *Alacha Gabcha* (Unequal Marriage), into English. Tsegaye's play, *Oda Oak Oracle*, was written in verse. The stream of consciousness writing in Dagnachew's *The Thirteenth Sun* was praised among critics. Solomon was at home writing essays and poetry both in Amharic and English.

Efforts to innovate Amharic poetry did not go without opposition, yet a powerful group of literary figures took up the challenge of introducing change. Mengistu Lemma, Tsegaye Gebre-Medhin, Gebre Kristos Desta and Solomon Deressa were at the forefront of secularizing language and experimenting with alternative versification. Notable writer Abe Gubegna and senior journalist Mulugeta Lule objected vociferously against this tampering with age-old principles of Amharic poetry, to little avail.[27] Poetry readings were common occurrence in the city.

Forging one fitting theoretical framework for new approaches in the visual, literary and performance arts of the 1960s is challenging, partly because authors, poets, playwrights and painters were busy in the act of creating. Although a sustained debate on a grand scale did not materialize, people like Mengistu Lemma, Tsegaye Gebre-Medhin, Yohannes Admasu and Solomon Deressa attempted to explain their understanding of Amharic literature in relation to the changes they were trying to institute.[28] Topics covered ranged from what constituted modern Amharic literature, what the role of the poet and author should be, the confines of rigid literary rules and the potential of combining Ethiopian languages and rhythms for broader comprehension. Sustained debate on the transformation of Ethiopian literature from traditional to modern, which began with the publication of an article by Mengistu Lemma in 1973, continued into the early 1980s with steady rejoinders being penned by Sahle Selassie Berhane-Mariam and Asfaw Damte in *Yekatit* magazine published in English.[29]

Painters were no less vocal when articulating their sense of place. Gebre Kristos Desta refused to be hemmed into a formulation that cast contemporary African artists as less "authentic" for using Western techniques in creating their works. He staunchly defended the need to develop new ways of seeing, arguing that the arts needed the same attention as other areas in a country's development.[30] Skunder Boghossian's internalization of African art profoundly influenced his approach, helping him to hone a new visual vocabulary that drew from Ethiopian traditions yet compositionally propelled it forward in unprecedented ways.[31]

The 1960s was also the decade that witnessed the erection of a number of beautiful buildings imbued with meaning and symbolism. Their construction gave Addis Ababa a cosmopolitan look. The city underwent three grand phases in its architecture. The first was around the second decade of the twentieth century when Indian architects built a series of impressive edifices. Greek and Armenian builders also erected residences and offices in imitation classical style. Italian presence in the 1930s initiated the second phase and its mark on the city's landscape is still widely apparent. The third phase occurred in the 1960s when a series of high-rise (by Addis standards) structures were built.

Unlike the accomplishments in other domains of the arts, expatriates dominated architecture in Addis Ababa. Nevertheless, the works had a visual impact. In the city center, the Municipality built a new hall with two sides that opened out as if to welcome and embrace the city and its people. This City Hall faced the railway station to which it was connected by a long and straight boulevard named after Winston Churchill. The Hilton Hotel, designed by the American firm Warner, Burns, Toan and Lunde, extensively borrowed motifs from the twelfth-century rock-hewn churches of Lalibela in northern Ethiopia. It was among the best architectural works of the time. Designed by the Paris firm of Henri Chomette, the head office of the Commercial Bank of Ethiopia, with its grand circular building reminiscent of a mud *tukul*, or traditional round house, became a fixture of the city (fig. 9). Modernist structures and spaces built in the period included the Ministry of Foreign Affairs building and Africa Hall, along with the National Palace and surrounding parks, all of which continue to grace the city today.

The dynamic synergy sparked by the confluence of talented visual, performance and literary artists was unduly disbanded by the revolution in 1974 by the Marxist Derg regime. Many artists left the country and were unable to sustain the creative pace away from home. Those who stayed struggled against the confines of communist aesthetics, initially attempting to adapt by tackling issues of change and revolution for the masses, but later abandoning the effort altogether. The Derg had its own ideas of popularizing performance arts and using theater and music to spread political message. To some extent, this served the purpose of making art accessible and of organizing neighborhood bands and dance troupes that competed for national airtime on radio and television.

The caliber of creativity and exchange could not, however, be reconstituted. Art as an end unto itself was considered capricious and superfluous, as the focus was on art's functionality in serving the cause. Gone was the intellectual fervor and breadth that inspired the florescence of the 1960s and provided the creative core around which artists communed.

It is a lasting testimony to the legacy of these golden years that up-and-coming performance and visual artists, as well as students of literature and poetry, continue to appreciate works by Skunder Boghossian, Gebre Kristos Desta, Tsegaye Gebre-Medhin, Mengistu Lemma and others. Electronic media regularly revisit their lives, dedicating long hours on radio and television to their works. The recent addition of Gebre Kristos Desta's name to the German Cultural Center (Goethe Institute); the 2006 publication of the first-ever catalogue of his paintings and an anthology of his poetry (almost twenty-six years after his passing); and the overwhelming outpouring of love and loss at the recent passing of Poet Laureate Tsegaye Gebre-Medhin (February 2006) indicate the far-reaching influence of these artists and their presence in popular memory. It is heartening to note that in countless ways big and small, the contemporary arts community is deeply engaged in honoring their struggles and milestones by looking back for inspiration to the florescence of the 1960s and the superbly seamless synthesis Ethiopian artists seem to have achieved.

Fig. 9   The head office of the Commercial Bank of Ethiopia in Addis Ababa designed by the Paris firm of Henri Chomette and constructed in the 1960s. Photograph by Rebecca Martin Nagy, 2006

1   Meaza Bekele, "A Study of Modern Education in Ethiopia: Its Foundations, Its Developments, Its Future with Emphasis on
    Primary Education" (Ph.D. Thesis, Columbia University, 1966), 75.

2   *Ibid.*, p. 78.

3   The name of University College of Addis Ababa was changed to Haile Selassie I University in 1961 and to Addis Ababa
    University in 1974.

4   Compiled from several sources: Abebe Fesseha, "Education and the Formation of the Modern Ethiopian State, 1896-1974"
    (Ph.D. Thesis, University of Illinois, Urbana-Champaign, 2000), 128.

5   Imperial Ethiopian Government Ministry of Education, *Elementary School Curriculum: Years I – VI* (Addis Ababa: Ministry
    of Education, 1948), 128-136.

6   *Ibid.*, 131-136.

7   *Ibid.*, 130.

8   *Ibid.*, 134.

9   *Ibid.*, 134.

10 Imperial Ethiopian Government Ministry of Education, *Secondary School Curriculum—Book I* (Addis Ababa: Ministry of
    Education, n.d.), 60.

11 *Ibid.*, 63.

12 Menilek II School has a distinguished place in Ethiopian history. Founded in 1907, it was the first public school in the
    country.

13 The lion created by sculptor Maurice Calka is still *in situ*. Calka was a well-established Parisian sculptor who had won
    the prestigious Premier Grand Prix de Rome.

14 Ashenafi received a BA degree from the University of Rochester's Eastman School of Music (1962) and the MA
    (1969) and Ph.D. (1971) degrees in ethnomusicology from Wesleyan University.

15 Wolde Ghebriel Tesfaye, "The Historical Development of the Yared Music School" (BA essay submitted to the
    Department of History of Addis Ababa University, 1983), 10-23.

16 *Ibid.*

17 *Afajeshign* (I am fighting for you) conveys a sense of chivalry in the fight for a beautiful woman and refers to
    Ethiopia during the Italian invasion. The word "mot" found in the title *Almotkum Biye Alwashim* (I won't pretend
    I have not perished or I won't pretend I have not been humiliated) literally means "death," but is used here to convey
    humiliation caused by the Italian invasion. Ethiopian men lost their wives, their land, their nation.

18 Francis Falcetto, *Abyssinie Swing* (Addis Ababa: Shama Books, 2001), 116.

19 *Gofere* is a hairstyle worn by young women.

20 This section on music draws partly from Zenebe Bekele's article originally published in Canada later reprinted in
    Addis Ababa. Zenebe Bekele, "*Ye'Etyopia Musika*," *Etyop* (A weekly Amharic paper) (Hedar 25, 1995 EC): 5.

21 Asfaw Damte, *Gebre Kristos Desta inna "Skunder" Boghossian, ande ande Tizitawoch*, [Gebre Kristos Desta and
    'Skunder' Boghossian—Reminiscences], *Journal of Ethiopian Studies Special Issue*, vol. 37 no. 2 (December
    2004): 105-121.

22 *Ibid.*:106.

23 In line with his interest in Egyptology and African ancient history, Tsegaye likens Skunder's artistic quest and even
    appearance, to Pharaoh Aknathon who instituted change to Egyptian civilization without shifting the foundation.
    Tsegaye posits Skunder as an original painter who forged a visual language that reached into the past to create a
    dynamic fusion that would speak to the present and the future.

24 Asfaw Damte, *Gebre Kristos Desta... Ibid.*: 108.

25 Berhane Meskel Dejene, "*Yese'ali Gebre Kristos Deta Yehiwot Tarik inna andand Gitmochu*" (BA Thesis, Institute of
    Language Studies, Addis Ababa University, 1982 EC), 84-86.

26 Asfaw Damte, *Gebre Kristos... Ibid.*: 112-115.

27 Abe Gubegna, "Meskot" (Berhanina Selam Printing Press, 1962 EC); Mulugeta Lule, *Kine Tibebat Sibedelu, Yezareyitu
    Ityopia* (Ginbot 17, 1960 EC).

28 See for example: Solomon Deressa, Introduction in *Lijinet, HaLe Metsahift* (Addis Ababa, 1963 EC) and *Solomon
    sile Solomon, Menen* (Tikimt 23, 1963 EC); Tsegaye Gebre Medhin, Introduction in *Isat Wey Abeba* (Berhanina Selam
    Printing Press, 1966 EC); Yohannes Admasu, *YeItyopia derasian yehibretesebun tikikiligna huneta meseretawi filagot
    yemeglets gideta alebachew* (n.d.).

29 See Mengistu Lemma, "From Traditional to Modern Literature in Ethiopia," *Zeitschrift fur Kulturaustausch*
    (Sonderausgabe, Addis Ababa, 1973); Sahle Selassie Berhane-Mariam, "Identification of National Literature,"
    Yekatit, vol. 5 no. 2 (December 1981); Asfaw Damte, "A 'National' Literature," *Yekatit*, vol. 5 no. 4 (June 1982); and
    Sahle Selassie Berhane-Mariam, "Talking of Language and Literature," *Yekatit*, vol. 6 no. 1 (September 1982).

30 See Sydney W. Head, "A Conversation with Gebre Kristos Desta," *African Arts,* vol. 2 no. 4, 1969, 20-24.

31 Anonymous, "Skunder Boghossian 'Afro-Metaphysics on Canvas," *Menen*, May 1966, 25-26.

Beauty and the Beast: Art and Dictatorship in Socialist Ethiopia, 1974-1991

Geta Mekonnen

Geta Mekonnen is an artist living and working in Addis Ababa. He graduated from the Addis Ababa Fine Arts School and earned a degree in fine arts from Bristol Polytechnic in England. As owner of Tewanney Studio, a graphic design firm, he has been instrumental in editing and publishing numerous catalogues documenting exhibitions of contemporary art in Addis Ababa. He has contributed essays to these and other publications, including an issue of *Revue Noire* in 1997 dedicated to Ethiopian and Eritrean Art, for which he was one of three coordinators.

> we who've been fragmented by serif and sound-bite
> who've covered our tracks back to the silence before the first scream
> whose tongues can no more move the weight of jaded words,
> we wait, though no one knows we are waiting…how come?
>
> *Solomon Deressa*[1]

When I set out to write this brief essay about a time we Ethiopians prefer to forget, I thought it was far enough away for detachment and close enough for clarity. I could not have been more wrong. Paradoxically, most of the material evidence no longer exists yet the experienced fear and intimidation, which has permanently shaped the collective psyche, linger on. We all seem to agree on unanimous silence, as if silence and denial keep us sane. If speaking only evokes and perpetuates grief and pain, in a place where grief and pain proliferate in infinitudes, only silence speaks out loudly enough. The deliberate eclipse of memory maintains the tinted landscape in balance with a tilted reality and silence defines a cynical perception of the present. Time seems to conspire with memory to debilitate consciousness and obscure the scars of the soul, disembodied by denial. As the Ethiopian saying goes, *Awko yeteggnan bikeseksut aysmam* (One who is feigning sleep cannot be awakened).

The birth of the military dictatorship in Ethiopia after the outburst of the popular revolution in 1974 was an atrocious outcome that no one had anticipated. Once it obtained absolute power and domination, the military dictatorship adopted socialism as an answer to the longstanding political, economic and cultural problems in which the country was mired. The choice soon proved wrong; the megalomaniac military dictatorship turned into a destructive beast that drove the country and its people into economic and psychological gridlock.

The failed coup against Emperor Haile Selassie in 1960 can be seen as a marking point after which the country was never to fall back into its former insomnia. The political situation was never stable again. From this time onward, the country was strangled by mass discontent, tense with an undercurrent of revolution. The politically conscious, observing the country's deteriorating agrarian-based economy and backward feudal administration, must have sensed the imminent arrival of the revolution. By the beginning of the 1970s, opposition to the feudal regime was not confined to a few discontented elite. Students, peasants, the armed forces and civil servants were also part of the constant rebellion against the complacent monarchy, which had no premonition of the magnitude of the crisis it faced.

It was against this political backdrop that artists and intellectuals begin to introduce the diverse influences of their foreign, modern post-war education. In the brief period from the mid-1960s to the mid-70s, the cultural life of the elite in Addis Ababa was superficially rich and sophisticated. Artists like Afewerk Tekle, Gebre Kristos Desta, Skunder Boghossian, Abdurahman Sherif and Tadesse Gizaw, upon returning from their respective foreign educations, brought with them an enthusiasm for the cultural influences and artistic movements of the time with all their exuberance and flamboyance. The new energy was shared by all the arts. Gebre Kristos' abstract expressionist paintings and his extreme productivity characterize the energy and the immediacy of this exciting time in modern Ethiopian history. And yet, its promise of a rebirth was beset with tension resulting from growing wealth for a handful and the overwhelming poverty of the country's millions.

The Addis Ababa Fine Arts School had been founded in 1957/58, only seven years after the establishment of the University College of Addis Ababa. Ale Felege Selam Heruy, founder of the school, returned from his studies in the United States determined to share what he had acquired abroad. For the first three years he worked in the Department of Research and Curriculum Development of the Ministry of Education and Fine Arts drawing illustrations for educational books. Then, at the age of 33, he established the Fine Arts School and become its first director. At the time the only practicing modern artist with formal training abroad was Afewerk Tekle, a young prodigy who had become an institution in his own right. Afewerk challenged the traditional artist's role as a servant of the church, exhibited his work and insisted on making a living solely from its sale, which was unheard of at the time. Afewerk, who studied in England and Italy in the 1940s, possessed intellectual and artistic dexterity together with the ability to use diverse styles and materials. His work includes easel paintings, mural paintings, sculpted monuments and monumental stained glass windows. It is not difficult to recognize the impact of Afewerk's artistic influence on the young people who flocked to the art classes of Ale Felege Selam Heruy's new school.

In 1961 the first scholarships awarded to graduates of the Fine Arts School were given to four talented students for study in the Soviet Union—Tadesse Belayneh, Worku Mammo, Tadesse Mamecha and Alemayehu Bonger. Two years later, Hailu Tsige and Taye Tadesse were sent to Poland, Ketsela Markos to Hungary and Alemayehu Bizuneh to France. Over the following years, several students were sent to both sides of the political divide, to Germany, France, England, Czechoslovakia, Hungary, the United States, Italy, Switzerland and Turkey. Out of the 119 students enrolled at the Fine Arts School during this period, a total of 54 students were sent abroad to study prior to the 1974 revolution that overthrew Haile Selassie. Of those, fourteen students went to the Eastern Bloc countries, whereas the others went to Western countries.

Gebre Kristos Desta returned from Germany in 1962 and Skunder Boghossian from France in 1966. Both were recruited to teach at the Fine Arts School, filling posts that were previously occupied by foreigners. Ale Felege Selam Heruy's idea to bring knowledge from across the world by sending students to diverse countries and political spheres of influence was the work of a visionary who wanted to create a new artistic tradition. Sculptors Tadesse Belayneh and Tadesse Mamecha returned in 1969 from the USSR. Painters Worku Mammo and Worku Goshu followed from the USSR and Poland, respectively. These young artists were sweepingly labeled "communists" by the authorities and treated with suspicion. From the second group to study abroad, Abdurahman Sherif returned from Germany in 1968 and began teaching graphic design. Gebre Kristos Desta and Skunder Boghossian shared a common grounding in modern art from their training in Western Europe in contrast to the other students returning from Eastern Bloc countries, who emphasized realistic drawing. The school was soon divided by tension and rivalry between teachers representing the different artistic emphases of the two political spheres. Under the new teachers, students such as Eshetu Tiruneh and Tadesse Mesfin were the first to absorb the academic style of the Soviet art schools. The style and content of their painting was clearly sympathetic with socialist realism.

Eshetu Tiruneh graduated in 1974 just prior to the revolution that would overthrow Haile Selassie. His controversial graduation work portrayed the terrible famine of 1974. This was a risky choice at the time since any subject critical of the Emperor's government was taboo. Gebre Kristos Desta was in favor of Eshetu's forceful critical approach, which he and fellow teachers Tadesse Belayneh and Tadesse Mamecha defended against Ale Felege Selam Heruy and others who were afraid the school would be seen as a breeding ground for young revolutionaries. Indeed, the students of the Fine Arts School in the early 1970s were part of a nation-wide students' movement that lead to the popular uprising of 1974. The backward feudal monarchy was floundering, with one hand clinging to the dark ages and the other desperately trying to find a magic wand of modernity to lift it into the twentieth century. For the young, the period was impregnated with tremendous hope. The uprising to bring an end to the centuries-old feudal rule was perceived as a prophetic radical vision to propel the country forward. But the forecast was erroneous, as historian Bahru Zewde has said,

Fig. 2 Gebre Kristos Desta
Design for theater poster
for *Struggle for Victory*, 1977
Ink and watercolor on paper
25 x 16 in. (63.5 x 40.6 cm.)
Collection of Mesfin Gebreyes
Oda, Addis Ababa

". . . the revolutionary spring was followed by the heavy and dark winter of terror."[2] The popular revolution was to be hijacked by the military junta, and soon the Marxist ideological orientation became the blueprint for the country's self destruction.

Until Tadesse Mesfin and Eshetu Tiruneh emerged, the country had no revolutionary artists (fig. 1). One revolutionary intellectual had this to say about their first exhibition: "A number of exhibitions have been held in post-revolutionary years where the works of art shown have spoken the language of the revolution and heralded the cry of the masses. These works of art were executed by young revolutionary artists like Tadesse Mesfin and Eshetu Tiruneh who had lived in oblivion during the last regime with their works piled in their *tukuls* [traditional round houses]. Among their paintings were: *The Workers*, *The Woman Cleaner*, *The Woman Wood Collector*, *The Shoe Shiner*, *The Beggar*, *The Victims of Famine*, *Just to Live*, etc. However, not all the works exhibited were, as would be expected, genuine works of revolutionary art."[3] At this time to be revolutionary was to be progressive, the essence of all enlightened youth. Tadesse Mesfin recently reminded me of a popular saying, "If you are not a communist at the age of 18 you are not normal and if you are a communist at the age of 40 you have a problem."[4] It is hard to say what would have happened in the artistic arena, had it not been for the terrible outcome of the revolution. One can only reflect on this period with a mix of sentimental yearning and frustration. The short-lived dynamic culture of pre-revolution Ethiopia was stifled in its nonage without any significant accomplishments.

I would classify Ethiopian art at the time leading up to the 1974 Revolution according to four categories: traditional art; modern art with African symbolism; abstract and expressionistic art; and academic realism. Traditional art encompasses three subgroups: 1) traditional artists producing Ethiopian Christian art, whose work includes church mural paintings, religious manuscripts and icons; 2) secular painters, whose paintings are rendered in the traditional technique of decorative flat compositions, characterized by the absence of perspective and naturalistic proportion; and 3) makers of magic scrolls, a kind of talismanic or healing art. Most of these traditional artists were trained in the apprenticeship system and had little or no formal education.

Modern art with African symbolism is a contemporary artistic expression inspired by African folklore, mythology, metaphor and calligraphy, whose best known practitioner was Skunder Boghossian. Despite its surrealist undertone, its relevance, artistic identity and creativity are rooted in its pan-African cultural consciousness, echoing pre-Christian healing art traditions and non-Christian visual culture. Elizabeth W. Giorgis has written that "Skunder considers himself a surrealist artist but one who is devoid of the paradigm of Western methodologies and Western constructs."[5] Included in this group are Zerihun Yetmgeta, Worku Goshu, Tibebe Terffa and Teshome Bekele.

Abstract and expressionistic artists were led by the artist/poet Gebre Kristos Desta, who returned from Germany bringing strong German expressionist and abstract expressionist influences. Unlike Skunder, Gebre Kristos was an outspoken advocate for a global mainstream culture, which was conjoined with modern industrial and scientific developments. In this category are painters Tadesse Gizaw, Abdurahman Sherif, Bisrat Bekele, Desta Hagos, Yohannes Gedamu and several others.

Academic realism is the style of Tadesse Mamecha, Worku Mamo and Tadesse Belayneh, all of whom trained in the Soviet Union, and was the official artistic style of the Fine Arts School during the seventeen years of the Derg regime. In fact, the school became the epicenter of the socialist propaganda machine. The impact of this new style was further strengthened by a stream of talented young artists returning from their seven-year course of study in various socialist countries. Academic realism includes two subgroups, which I identify as "socialist realism" and "social realism." Socialist realism includes various kinds of propaganda art, such as posters, banners and other ephemera, as well as monumental painting and sculpture that portrays aspects of socialist philosophy or important historical events in lasting materials such as fresco, mosaic, oil on canvas or stone. The sole purpose of socialist realist art is the advancement of socialist ideology. Social realist art, on the other hand, depicts subjects of social concern in a realistic style but without the direct influence of socialist political ideology.

A socialist state has no tolerance for a multitude of artistic styles and socialist realism became the prescribed style of the Derg regime, replacing both the ancient Christian traditions of Ethiopia and the imported Western modernist styles that were viewed by the Marxist government as bourgeois and degenerate. A nihilistic frenzy to destroy any legacy of the past and to create a new culture led to burning books and vandalizing monuments. Tadesse Belayneh, one of the first artists to study in the Soviet Union, told me of an incident when he was working at the Somali border. He was recalled to Addis Ababa and ordered to remove the crown from the large Lion of Judah monument adjacent to the National Theater, a symbol of the reign of Haile Selassie. The situation forced the artist to choose between his survival and his professional integrity. Having bravely chosen the latter, he was called before a senior official to explain why he refused to remove the crown. In the end, the official accepted the Soviet-trained artist's arguments regarding the importance of preserving heritage and history. The monument still stands intact as does the integrity of the artist.[6]

Socialist realism was a direct cultural import that accompanied the radical political shift to socialism in Ethiopia and was copied directly from its Soviet prototype. Recognizing art as the backbone of the socialist revolution, Ethiopian socialist art critic Seyoum Wolde published in 1980 his *Meseretawi marxawi yesine tibeb dinigagewoch, yesocialist Kinet Acher Memeria* (Fundamental Marxist Principles of Art, Concise Rules for Socialist Art), in which he outlined the essential concepts and guidelines for the production and purpose of art under socialism. He observed: "Based on historical objectivity and reality, art should reflect life in socialist development, to envision and guide society to a higher standard of socialist existence…inspired by this clear motivation, art is used to speed up the progress of socialist revolution, strengthening socialist existence and creating a new society formed with completeness of spiritual beauty in harmony with perfect physical appearance and beauty."[7]

Between 1974 and 1991, all media and production facilities as well as performance and exhibition venues were under the direct control of the government and censorship was strictly applied to all publications, performances and exhibitions.

The involuntary participation of artists and art students was a common practice in the production of posters, banners and stamps bearing propaganda images of the "glorification of the proletariat." Even heavyweights such as Afewerk Tekle and Gebre Kristos Desta did not escape such orders (fig. 2). The role of the artist under a dictatorship is to create art, the most effective psychological mechanism for promulgating propaganda for the manipulation of the people. The artist was always on standby, in complete subservience to the system in order to avoid the fateful consequences of being labeled a bourgeois or degenerate artist.

By 1977 the revolution saw Ethiopia's educated youth divided into various political activist and militant groups that waged urban guerrilla warfare against the military rule of the Derg. The Derg unleashed the brutal Red Terror campaign in response to this urban youth resistance movement. Derg Chairman Mengistu Haile Mariam vowed at a public rally to conquer the enemies of the revolution and accented his words by smashing a bottle of blood, to the shock and dismay of millions. According to Human Rights Watch, the Red Terror was "one of the most systematic uses of mass murder by the state ever witnessed in Africa."[8] It eliminated tens of thousands of young people and terrorized the whole population, establishing the military dictatorship as an unchallenged absolute authority. From this point on there was increasingly less resistance in the urban centers in contrast to a growing insurgency in the north of the country, as well as in the Diaspora. The use of violence and intimidation continued until the overthrow of the regime in 1991. Many artists were imprisoned, tortured and a few were killed. The indiscriminate nature of this terror is revealed in one shocking example recently recounted to me. A young, deaf art student was walking home minutes after the set curfew time, when he was ordered to stop by the armed revolutionary guard. When he didn't respond after three calls, he was shot several times in the back and killed on the spot.[9] Such harrowing stories from this time are common.

Seyoum Wolde's fundamental principles of socialist realism were applied at the Fine Arts School. Rules and guidelines were issued regarding the training of art students as well as strict procedures to direct the production of graduation works by final-year students. A list of acceptable

Fig. 3   Assefa Wolde Mariam
The Call, 1980
Woodcut
37 x 58 1/4 in. (94 x 148 cm.)
Collection of the School
of Fine Arts and Design

top to bottom

Fig. 4   Gebre Luel Gebre Mariam
          Searching Squad, 1979
          Oil on canvas
          72 3/4 x 83 3/4 in. (185 x 213 cm.)
          Collection of the School of Fine Arts
          and Design, Addis Ababa University

Fig. 5   Abraham Gebre
          On Duty, 1979
          Oil on canvas
          55 x 58 3/4 in. (140 x 149 cm.)
          Collection of the School of
          Fine Arts and Design,
          Addis Ababa University

themes for the creation of socialist art was issued: 1) glorification of the proletarian struggle and its achievements (fig. 3); 2) patriotism and heroes of the revolution, and the military defending the mother land (fig. 4); 3) socialist farmers engaged in communal work, the equality of women and women at work or as mothers (fig. 5); 4) humanity defined by work and depictions of people at work (fig. 6); 5) historical heroes and martyrs of the people in anti-imperialist and anti-capitalist struggle (fig. 7); and 6) depiction of cultural festivities and the cultural life of marginalized societies and ethnic groups. Students were required to work only from the list and choices from the top of the list were encouraged by the administration and faculty. Often the first two options were chosen by technically inferior students and opportunists. In contrast, the second two choices were fairly acceptable for many students because the subjects allowed for a poetic and metaphorical approach. The national hero engaged in an anti-imperialist struggle was an attractive subject for many ambitious young artists. Ambiguous subject matter was preferred by many conscientious yet cautious students. It is not a coincidence that most of the heroes chosen by the most talented students were martyrs.

As the situation under the Derg deteriorated, many artists left the country, including Gebre Kristos Desta, who went to the United States in 1980. The stifling political situation and the persistent criticism were suffocating for their work. For many young artists the situation was even worse; their apparent political involvement put their lives at risk. Some artists who wanted to stay in the country had to accept and embrace the socialist ideology, or at least pretend to do so. In Esseye G. Medhin's words, some were "encouraged to conform by the system of rewards and privileges through commissions. Many, like respected artist Abdul Rahman M. Sherif, saw this sort of compensation as a 'fulfilment genuine enough, of their professional ideals.'"[10] Abdurahman, as the director of the art school, was in no position to resist the demands imposed on him and his school. One socialist critic observed: "The fate of the celebrated artist of the pre-revolutionary days at first was a difficult one. They were attacked for their past works and they had to defend themselves and to catch up with the progress of the revolution. Afewerk Tekle,

who was most affected in this respect, never gave up or set aside his brush. Instead, with the rare discipline and diligence that characterizes this internationally famous artist, he set out to create works that depict the revolution and the Ethiopia he loves. The result was rewarding, and Afewerk, whose huge three-metre by five-metre work, *The Victory of Ethiopia through Work, Productivity and Struggle*…now hangs at the Patriot Center in Debre Zeit, has regained his former enviable position…"[11] The monumental art project at the Patriot Art Center involved a number of well-known artists including Tadesse Gizaw, Bisrat Bekele, Bekele Abebe, Ale Felege Selam Heruy, Tadesse Belayneh, Tadesse Mamecha and others. None of them was paid a single dollar for his work. It was a clear official order, which they all accepted in order to spare their lives from the trigger-happy cadres.

The tenth anniversary of the revolution in 1984 was the greatest spectacle the country had ever seen. The details and resources that went into the celebration were bewildering—the decoration of the city (often under the supervision of North Korean artists) and manifestations of military might. Large billboards at Revolution Square featured the Socialist Trinity of Marx, Engels and Lenin on one side and a giant portrait of Mengistu Haile Mariam on the other. Artists employed in government offices as well as art students were called on to participate in months-long preparations for a meager four birr a day allowance. No one who was moderately skilled could escape without painting a portrait of Mengistu, which were often criticized by the cadres—the skin was too dark, the lips were too big—and they demanded a repainting.[12] It was against the backdrop of this show of bravado that the humiliating news of the 1984 famine broke out. Outside Ethiopia the government earned universal condemnation for its inability and unwillingness to deal with the famine that affected millions of Ethiopians.

In Ethiopia, socialist realism never really took root outside of the Fine Arts School. After graduation, students struggled to shed the rigorous socialist training they had received. Unable to pursue any other forms of expression, most graduates practiced their profession very little as a form of passive resistance. Many remember resentfully the seventeen years under

the socialist dictatorship, when everything they did was scrutinized by the state. As a result, there are few works of art that capture the essence of this oppressive era. Only a handful of artists including Zerihun Yetmgeta, Worku Goshu, Tibebe Terffa and Teshome Bekele, continued to show their work during the socialist era, notably at the French, Italian and German cultural centers, which were nominally outside government control. Although these artists were not openly banned from producing semi-abstract symbolic art, the content of their exhibitions was thoroughly censored. Often works were rejected on the basis of ambiguous meaning and titles were changed to avoid double entendre. For Ethiopian artists, such changes were significant, for the use of double meanings, described as "wax and gold," is central to Ethiopian tradition. Wax refers to the overt or surface meaning, while gold refers to the hidden, deeper meaning. Once in a discussion among artists the question was raised why there weren't any artworks that challenged the Derg. In the profound words of Mesfin Habtemariam, "In those days, surviving was an art."[13]

The Derg regime only managed to substitute one form of totalitarian dictatorship for another. Mengistu Haile Mariam behaved like any other king with absolute power and even lived in Emperor Menilek's palace. The musician changed but not the music. In the seventeen years of its existence, the Derg succeeded only in creating an intricate network of politicized institutions instrumental to its oppressive regime. With the downfall of the Derg in 1991, artists were finally free from explicit influence and control, free to explore their individual tendencies and directions. However, as Esseye G. Medhin has observed, although the artistic situation of the 1970s and 1980s dissolved once and for all, the new generation of artists continued to be affected by the tumult of the recent past. In his words: "The mindset as to what to do and how to define what is done still lingers."[14] Over the last thirty years since the 1974 Revolution, artists have often wandered through different approaches in an attempt to find meaning for their artistic skill and creativity. Hoping to piece together the puzzle of their identity, most young artists are preoccupied with the question of "Ethiopianness" in their work. This is captured in the contemplative words of Hiruy Arefayne: "What does it mean to be an Ethiopian artist in the midst of uncertain [sic] of what it means to be Ethiopian?"[15]

The beast died long ago and the skin should be hanging on the wall as in the days of our ancestors. The scar on our memory should be healed, but the legacy of silence is yet to be broken. We must agree that this creative inertia is a product of social reticence born of deeply ingrained fear and denial. We cannot continue to recoil to the distant past to find consolation, overlooking the present and the recent past. If we are to go forward, we must understand the recent past and reflect on the present. The rear view mirror is only a reference. We must remember that the past is made here in the present and in the future.

top to bottom

Fig. 6   Fitsum Admasse
          Harmony, 1981
          Oil on canvas
          44 1/2 x 68 in. (113 x 173 cm.)
          Collection of the School of
          Fine Arts and Design, Addis
          Ababa University

Fig. 7   Samuel Sharew,
          Victory Overseas, 1986
          Oil on canvas
          45 3/4 x 54 1/4 in. (116 x 138 cm.)
          Collection of the School
          of Fine Arts and Design,
          Addis Ababa University

1   From an unpublished manuscript, "The Poem Unsheathed," entrusted to the author by Solomon Deressa.
2   Bahru Zewde, *A History of Modern Ethiopia 1855–1991* (Addis Ababa University Press, 1991, second edition, 2001), 229.
3   Aleme Eshete, *The Cultural Situation in Socialist Ethiopia* (Paris: United Nations Educational, Scientific and Cultural
     Organization, 1982), 28.
4   Personal conversation with the artist, September 2006.
5   Elizabeth W. Giorgis, "Art in a Changing World: Trends in Contemporary African Art and Diaspora Ethiopian Art,"
     Proceedings of the Sixth International Conference on the History of Ethiopian Art, Addis Ababa, November 5–8, 2002
     (Addis Ababa: Institute of Ethiopian Studies, Addis Ababa University, 2003), 286.
6   Personal conversation with the artist, September 2006.
7   Seyoum Wolde, *Fundamental Marxist Principles of Art, Concise Rules for Socialist Art* (Self-published by Seyoum Wolde,
     Addis Ababa, 1980) Translation by Geta Mekonnen.
8   Andrew Rice, "The Long Interrogation," *New York Times Magazine*, June 4, 2006.
9   This episode was relayed to the author by Tadesse Belayneh, former director of the Addis Ababa Fine Arts School, during an
     interview conducted in 2006.
10   Esseye G. Medhin, "Addis Ababa Art Scene Revisited," *Ethiopian BIR*, vol. 4, no. 2.
11   Aleme Eshete, *ibid*.
12   I recall one incident when Mesfin Habtemariam and I were producing a mural in for the tractor factory in Nazret, a
     town south of Addis Ababa, which included a large portrait of Mengistu. The night before the inauguration of the
     facility one cadre appeared and insisted that the chairman appeared too dark and must be corrected. We were lifted up
     on a crane with all our tools and pretended to paint, but we only wet the portrait with water and asked if it were
     acceptable then. Ashamed of his ignorance the cadre agreed without hesitation that the face was now correct. There
     are many anecdotes of this nature that can not be included in an essay of this length.
13   Conversation with the artist, 1997.
14   Eseye G. Medhin, *ibid*.
15   Hiruy Arefe-Ayne, "The Shared Symbols," *Revue Noire*, vol. 24, 1997, 35.

Rebecca Martin Nagy is director of the Samuel P. Harn Museum of Art and an affiliate member of the graduate faculty of the School of Art and Art History at the University of Florida in Gainesville. She was previously associate director of education and curator of African art at the North Carolina Museum of Art. She holds a doctorate in art history from the University of North Carolina in Chapel Hill, where she was an adjunct faculty member from 1988 to 2002. She has received Fulbright fellowships for study in Germany and Ghana, and has published in the areas of medieval art, biblical archaeology and American and African modern and contemporary art.

Venues for Contemporary Art

Any visitor to Addis Ababa who expresses a sincere desire to see the work of contemporary Ethiopian artists will soon be introduced to a lively network of artists, group studios, collectors, exhibition venues and sales galleries. The local art scene is vibrant and energetic despite numerous challenges and significant obstacles with which artists and arts administrators must contend.

The Addis Ababa University School of Fine Arts and Design (SFAD) is a significant cultural and educational resource for the community, offering weekend art classes for children and evening art classes for adults as well as an extensive summer art program for children. For a small fee people can enroll in these classes taught by SFAD faculty, who supplement their incomes by teaching in extension programs. One successful young Ethiopian painter, Fikru Gebre Mariam, who divides his time between Paris and Addis Ababa, credits the Saturday art classes that he attended for four years as a child with his decision to study at the SFAD and to pursue a career as an artist.[1]

The SFAD gallery space is the venue for exhibitions of work by current faculty and students and featured guest artists as well as installations drawn from the school's extensive holdings of work by former faculty and students since the time of the institution's founding in 1957/58 (fig. 1). Educational programming in conjunction with exhibitions includes lectures, panel discussions and gallery talks. Guest curators are sometimes invited to organize shows for the SFAD gallery. Meskerem Assegued, with an academic background in anthropology, is active in Addis Ababa and internationally as an arts administrator and independent curator. In 2006 she organized for the SFAD an exhibition of work by contemporary Mayan artists from Mexico's Yucatan region, including Ernesto Novelo, who held an artist's residency at the Zoma Contemporary Art Center Meskerem directs. Novelo's residency and the related exhibition provided a rare opportunity for artists and art students in Addis Ababa to see and learn about the work of a contemporary artist from another part of the world. One of the serious limitations of the exhibition offerings at the city's museums, galleries and alternative venues is that, with rare exceptions, only work of Ethiopian artists is shown. Unless they have the means to travel outside the country, local artists have few opportunities to experience work by international artists firsthand.

Fig. 1   Exhibition gallery in the administrative and classroom building of the School of Fine Arts and Design, Addis Ababa University Photograph by Rebecca Martin Nagy, 2002

For viewing work by Ethiopian modern and contemporary artists, some venues exist and new ones are being developed. The National Museum of Ethiopia has a modest collection of paintings and sculpture by twentieth century artists, many of which have come into the museum as gifts from the artists themselves. The museum is seriously understaffed in key areas such as curatorial, registration, conservation and installation design. Furthermore, there are almost no funds for acquisitions, conservation or mounting exhibitions from the permanent collection. In recent years under the leadership of its director, anthropologist Mamitu Yilma, the museum has mounted group shows by young and emerging artists, including students of the SFAD, in underutilized buildings on the museum's grounds (fig. 2). Happily, the museum is adding a new building for art storage, conservation and study that will also free space in the main museum building for exhibitions. With collections ranging from paleontology to contemporary art, the museum is a popular destination for student groups, local citizens and foreign visitors.

The Institute of Ethiopian Studies (IES) of Addis Ababa University has extensive holdings and well-conceived ethnographic installations as well as attractive displays of the art of the Ethiopian Orthodox Church tradition, and nineteenth and twentieth-century folk art. But the IES does not typically show the work of contemporary artists other than church, folk and self-taught artists.

In 2006 a major new venue for the exhibition of contemporary art opened at Addis Ababa University as a partnership between the university and the German Cultural Institute (Goethe Institute). A historic building from Haile Selassie's time was renovated and expanded as the new location of the Institute's offices, classrooms, library and other facilities, including a handsome gallery for art exhibitions, and to house a collection of some thirty paintings and works on paper by Gebre Kristos Desta (fig. 3). The artist studied and lived in Cologne, Germany from 1957 to 1962 before returning to Addis Ababa where he taught at the Fine Arts School from 1963 to 1980. In his memory and honor the Goethe Institute's facility is named the "Goethe-Institut Addis Abebe Gebrekristos Desta Center." The building is handsomely detailed, beautifully furnished and well-equipped with computers and other technological resources. However, admirers of Gebre Kristos have expressed keen disappointment that his work is not always accessible to visitors. When the center's single gallery space is being used for other art and historical exhibitions, Gebre Kristos' paintings are stored in offices and conference rooms where visitors are unable to see and study them.

For years, certainly since the overthrow of the Derg regime in 1991, artists, academics, cultural and arts administrators and others have dreamed of a museum of modern and contemporary art that would collect work by Ethiopian artists and

exhibit their work as well as that of international artists. The opening of the Gebrekristos Desta Center has perhaps offered new hope that this dream may become a reality in the foreseeable future. A public-private partnership similar to that forged between Addis Ababa University and the Addis Ababa Goethe Institute may be the best vehicle for founding such a museum, given that government support and funding for cultural institutions is limited.

A case in point is a proposed palace museum in Addis Ababa. A government-appointed committee has been working in recent months on a proposal to open a museum at Haile Selassie's Jubilee Palace, which houses extensive collections associated with his long reign—royal regalia, decorative arts, diplomatic gifts and so on—as well as a large collection of paintings produced during the same period (1930-1974). The proposed museum would include furnished rooms in the palace, installations from the collections, a gallery for changing exhibitions of contemporary art, and restored gardens and grounds. Indeed, a Japanese garden has already been restored through a partnership with the Japanese government, but is not open to the public. Although this Jubilee Palace museum certainly would hold wide appeal for Ethiopians and foreigners alike, adequate funding to realize the project may not be forthcoming.

In the absence of government-sponsored venues for contemporary art, foreign cultural institutes such as the German Cultural Institute, the Alliance Ethio-Française and the Italian Cultural Institute play a major role in hosting exhibitions by local artists and providing educational programs such as

top to bottom

Fig. 2   Achamyeleh Debela (far right) speaking with art students from the School of Fine Arts and Design at an exhibition of work by young artists at the National Museum of Ethiopia. Photograph by Rebecca Martin Nagy, 2002

Fig. 3   Exhibition gallery with paintings by Gebre Kristos Desta at the Goethe-Institut Addis Abebe Gebrekristos Desta Center. Photograph by Rebecca Martin Nagy, 2006

top to bottom

Fig. 4   Guests at the opening
          reception for an exhibition at
          the Alliance Ethio-Française
          in Addis Ababa. Photograph
          by Rebecca Martin Nagy, 2005

Fig. 5   Asni Gallery in Addis Ababa.
          Photograph by Rebecca
          Martin Nagy, 2001

lectures, panels and round tables. Indicative of the increasing vitality of the local contemporary art scene is the tremendous enthusiasm and energy generated by exhibitions at these venues. The crowds at art openings are a mix of Ethiopians and foreign residents, old and young, including many students and recent graduates from the School of Fine Arts and Design. These gatherings provide opportunities for young artists to mix with older successful artists, network and seek advice.

The gallery space at the Alliance Ethio-Française, designed by architect and Addis Ababa University Professor Fasil Giorgis, is a favorite venue for solo and group shows by Addis Ababa's leading artists (fig. 4). In conjunction with these shows, exhibiting artists speak about their work, discuss issues of common interest, and respond to questions and comments from the audience. Painter Yohannes Gedamu, who returned to Addis Ababa in 1997/98 after living and working for seventeen years in Cologne, Germany, is a leading figure in organizing lectures and panel discussions on contemporary art for the Goethe Institute. Thus, although young artists have few opportunities to see work by international artists from other parts of the world, they increasingly have occasions to see work by Ethiopian artists and engage in discussion of issues important to them.

In addition to the cultural centers, there are some alternative exhibitions spaces and commercial galleries that are making significant contributions to the Addis Ababa art scene by staging group and solo shows and by representing Ethiopian artists and promoting their work to the small but growing group of patrons collecting contemporary art in the city. Asni Gallery, which occupies a beautifully renovated nineteenth-century house, shows work by young, emerging and established artists (fig. 5). Its founder and proprietor, Konjit Seyoum, has also reached out to children by offering Saturday art classes. She acknowledges that the gallery is largely a labor of love and that, despite a good record of sales from shows, it is not self-sustaining or profitable. On some occasions, she organizes exhibitions in which none of the work is for sale, as was the case, for instance, when she borrowed works from private collections in Addis Ababa to stage a one-person show of paintings by modern master Skunder Boghossian. Although he is greatly revered and widely imitated by younger Ethiopian

artists, most of Skunder's works are in collections outside Ethiopia and are thus inaccessible to the majority of people in Addis Ababa.

Meskerem Assegued seeks contributions from private donors and receives funding from some of the foreign embassies in the city to run the Zoma Contemporary Art Center's artist residency program, artist and critic lectures and other educational programs and to mount site-specific installations and group and solo exhibitions in various venues in the city. Many of the young artists whose work Meskerem shows are graduates of the School of Fine Arts and Design, which she credits with providing these young artists an excellent foundation in the fine arts. Meskerem is also building an art reference library for Zoma Contemporary Art Center, which is available for use by artists and other researchers. She is raising funds to acquire a permanent facility to house the Zoma Art Center, its library and various programs.

Other galleries in Addis Ababa are more commercial in nature, featuring decorative arts along with the work of a few highly successful painters. St. George Interior Decorations and Art Gallery, for example, is known for its unique furniture and rare Ethiopian jewelry and artifacts. Owner Saba Alene has gained a reputation for her exquisite designs that incorporate traditional motifs such as *harag* (interlace). Saba has developed a niche by combining her talent as a designer and a businesswoman. She also represents well-known Ethiopian artists who live in Addis Ababa such as Zerihun Yetmgeta and Mezgebu Tessema and the Diaspora, including Wosene Kosrof. Chilota Studio is another commercial gallery that showcases high-quality crafts while also representing some notable artists, such as painter Lulseged Retta. Artists Barbara and Worku Goshu own and manage Goshu Art Gallery, which features their paintings along with handicrafts from Ethiopia and elsewhere. They make the gallery available to young artists at no cost. Most of the collectors buying art from these galleries are foreigners living or passing through Addis Ababa, although a few local business people and academics are beginning to build significant collections. Established artists also exhibit their work at the city's principal luxury hotels, the Sheraton and Hilton. Foreign residents of the city frequently attend these shows and sales can be brisk.

The art centers and galleries described above are exemplary in their commitment to showing and promoting the work of serious artists. Konjit Seyoum and Meskerem Assegued have demonstrated particular commitment to showing and supporting the work of young emerging artists. Unfortunately, there are numerous galleries and shops in Addis Ababa that undermine the efforts of serious gallerists and curators by showing paintings alongside cheap trinkets and souvenirs and by encouraging young artists to turn out inferior copies or works in the style of well-known painters to sell to foreigners. In a city where there are still relatively few local collectors and patrons buying contemporary art, young artists understandably are tempted to forsake serious development of their own distinctive work in order to make work that will sell. Some adopt a practical approach whereby they quickly produce paintings with wide popular appeal as a way to earn income so that they can devote studio time to experiment and produce serious work for exhibition or, occasionally, on commission.

Artists' Alliances and Group Studios

Artists' alliances have grown in popularity over the fifteen years since the fall of the Derg regime. One of the first such groups was the *Awtar* or Dimension Group founded by artists Geta Mekonnen and Bekele Mekonnen (not related) with six other artists in 1995. The belief shared by its members "that harmony through diversity creates a dynamic that is crucial to the creative process," is reflected in the group's name, which they explain in the forward to their first group exhibition catalogue from 1995:

> The word 'dimension' was translated from the Amharic word 'Awtar' which means: a tightened string of a harp, a guy rope of a tent, or a ray of the sun. Each string of the harp creates its own sound but together with other strings it creates melody. One guy rope does not hold the tent straight but together with others it can support a shelter. Thus, the idea is for each artist to bring their individual light so that together a brighter light is created.[2]

A major Dimension initiative was the publication of a catalogue for each exhibition as a way of promoting scholarly and critical discussion of the artists' work and providing permanent documentation of the shows. Although the group has not formally disbanded, its last exhibition and publication were in 2001 and there are no plans at present to revitalize the program.

Increasingly, younger artists, most of them recent graduates of the School of Fine Arts and Design, are forming group studios in order to afford work and exhibition space, mount group shows and host artists' forums and roundtables. Although they sometimes print flyers to promote their shows, these studio groups seldom have the financial means to publish brochures or catalogues. Among the more established group studios are Saron Studio and Habesha Art Studio. In 2004 they jointly organized a "Friendship Painting Exhibition" at Saron Studio, for which a small illustrated color brochure was printed. The Habeshas, as the five male members of the Habesha Studio identify themselves, commented in the brochure that "working in groups allows them to share several things including ideas which they wouldn't have been able to working individually."[3]

One of the newest group studios is Nubia Studio, with three men and two women sharing studio and exhibition space in a rented house (fig. 6). All are recent graduates of the SFAD. Nubia Studio does not print flyers or brochures, but rather draws crowds for the openings of its shows primarily through word-of-mouth publicity. Remarkably, a number of the artists in these group studios are able to survive through sale of their work. The majority of them are painters, although some work with sculpture or mixed media. Tesfahun Kibru, whose work is included in this exhibition, is one of the most interesting recent graduates of the SFAD working with assemblage sculpture. Tesfahun, along with two other male artists who graduated from the SFAD, belongs to the New Art Space Studio near Ras Makonnen Bridge. Painter Tamrat Gezahegne, a former member of this studio group who is also included in the present exhibition, moved into a private studio in 2006.

Fig. 6   Artists of Nubia Studio, left to right: Kerima Ahmed Mohammed, Yonas Sahle Belayneh, Merikokeb Birhanu and Dereje Demissie W/Georgis. Not pictured is Samuel Endalamaw Asfaw. Photograph by Achamyeleh Debela, 2006

Fig. 7   The library building of the School
of Fine Arts and Design, Addis
Ababa University. Photograph by
Rebecca Martin Nagy, 2005

Obstacles and Challenges

Other than occasional catalogues published
in conjunction with exhibitions, such as those
produced by the Dimension Group over a period
of seven years, there are few vehicles in Ethiopia
for publication of historical or critical writings
about contemporary art. A noteworthy and rare
occurrence was the 2006 publication of a book
on the career and oeuvre of Gebre Kristos Desta,
produced to mark the occasion of the opening
of the Goethe-Institut Addis Abebe Gebrekristos
Desta Center with an exhibition of the paintings
housed there.[4] At the same time, an edition of Gebre
Kristos Desta's poetry in Amharic and English
translation was published, with scholarly essays.[5]
Such volumes are definitely the exception to the
rule. There are only a few trained art historians
in Addis Ababa and no practicing art critics.
Although serious art criticism is virtually absent,
journalistic interest in artists and exhibitions is
strong and local media provide good coverage of
exhibitions and related events.

The dearth of books and journals offering historical
and critical analysis of Ethiopian contemporary
art is paralleled by an almost complete absence
on newsstands and even in academic libraries of
art periodicals and other publications. Artists

who are unable to travel abroad have almost no
opportunity to read about contemporary artists
and exhibitions in other parts of Africa and the
rest of the world. Although the SFAD has a new
library building, the school has limited resources
to acquire books and none for subscriptions to
art journals and newspapers, a situation which
results in isolation of university students from
major trends and developments in the art world
outside Addis Ababa (fig. 7). Although still limited,
internet access has improved greatly at the SFAD
and at other venues, such as the computer center
at the Goethe Institute, providing a connection to
artists in other parts of the world.

For a variety of reasons, painting remains the
dominant art form and the medium of choice for
most art students, as has been true in Ethiopia for
centuries. It is ironic that in Addis Ababa, as in the
entire country, there is no art supply store or any
other source of art materials for painters and other
artists, who often depend on friends traveling
abroad or foreign visitors to purchase and bring
in paints, brushes and other high-quality materials.
On the other hand, faculty and students at the
SFAD have become quite creative in identifying
local sources for materials that meet their basic
needs. Paper is purchased from printing companies
and gesso for priming canvases from the building
construction industry, while house paints are
used in lieu of tubes of oil or acrylic paints. Clay
for sculpting can be dug locally, and concrete is
an inexpensive and readily obtainable medium
for monumental sculpture. Young artists such
as Tesfahun Kibru and Elias Sime use found and
recycled materials, often purchased at the Mercato,
Addis Ababa's sprawling central market. Until such
time as enterprising entrepreneurs capitalize on
the need for art supply stores, art gallery owners
should be encouraged to provide a much-needed
service to local artists by carrying a basic line of
art supplies.

The majority of artists, especially recent graduates
of the SFAD and other young artists, cannot afford
to travel, even to sites of historic and artistic
interest in distant areas of Ethiopia much less
outside the country's borders. Only a fortunate few
obtain scholarships or financial assistance to study
abroad. The situation was quite different for their
professors, the second generation associated with
the School of Fine Arts and Design, many of whom

studied in the former Soviet Union and other Eastern Bloc countries during the years of the Derg regime (1974–1991). Although these artists were trained in conservative academies in the socialist realist style, their studies abroad provided wide exposure to European art in museums and historic buildings that their students today see only in reproduction.

Among the established artists working in Addis Ababa today, several travel frequently to other African countries, Europe and the United States where they hold residencies, attend workshops or mount exhibitions of their work. Lulseged Retta and Elizabeth Hapte Wold, for example, recently had exhibitions of their paintings at galleries in the United States, in Los Angeles and Washington respectively.[6] In 2006 sculptor Bekele Mekonnen had a residency at the Maryland Institute College of Art, having recently had a similar appointment at Bowling Green State University (2003). Bekele has also had major exhibitions in Florence, Italy (2002) and Kuopio, Finland (1992). In 2006 painter Behailu Bezabih had an artist's residency in Kenya, having previously held residencies in the United Kingdom (2005), Germany (2004), Uganda (2004), South Africa (2001) and, again, Kenya (2000). These and other artists who travel and work abroad return to Ethiopia and share their experiences and insights with others through lectures, panels and roundtables and interviews in the media. For most of the younger generation of artists such experiences are unattainable. Fikru Gebre Mariam, who graduated from the Fine Arts

School in 1995, is one exception. He is represented by galleries in France and has sold enough work there and in the United States to build a house in Addis Ababa so that he can divide his time between France and Ethiopia. Another exception is Elias Sime, who was one of two Ethiopian artists in the 2004 Dak'Art biennale de l'art africain contemporain in Dakar, Senegal. His work was selected for an installation at Peter Sellars' New Crowned Hope Festival in Vienna in 2006.[7] Ethiopian and foreign collectors have purchased many of Elias' works and, like Fikru, he is building a house in Addis Ababa.

Geta Mekonnen wrote in an essay published in *Revue Noire* in 1997, that "... contemporary Ethiopian artists face a great challenge as visionaries of the new Ethiopia. They strive to create a new image and forge a new identity; to build a bridge between the old and the new."[8] Just as a bridge between the old and the new is important for young artists, so is the possibility for meaningful participation in international cultural exchange while maintaining a solid grounding in their Ethiopian heritage. Despite the problems and challenges faced by artists in Addis Ababa, the positive changes of the last decade have resulted in many new opportunities for both established and emerging artists. Although not without struggle and hardship, they are contributing to a new florescence of the arts in Addis Ababa. Perhaps it will rival the legendary "Addis Spring" of the 1960s.

1   Conversation with the artist, September 2003.
2   *Dimension Group (Awtar): Exhibition of Eight Ethiopian Artists*, May 23–June 2, 1995, at the Alliance Ethio-Française, exhibition catalogue, p. 3.
3   *Friendship Painting Exhibition*, Saron Studio, Addis Ababa, December 16–25, 2004, exhibition brochure, p. 1.
4   Elizabeth W. Giorgis, ed., *Gebre Kristos Desta: The Painter Poet* (Institute of Ethiopian Studies, Addis Ababa University, 2006).
5   Heran Sereke-Brhan, ed., *Expansive Pathway . . . Lifetime Traveler: Gebre Kristos Desta, An Anthology of Poetry*. (Institute of Ethiopian Studies, Addis Ababa University, 2006).
6   Lulseged had a show most recently at Addis Art Gallery in Los Angeles in 2005. Elisabeth Habte Wold is represented by Parish Gallery in Georgetown, Washington, D.C., where her most recent show was mounted in 2004.
7   Elias' work was selected for an exhibition titled "Green Flame," curated for the festival by Peter Sellars and Meskerem Assegued.
8   Geta Mekonnen, "Currents of Change," *Revue Noire*, vol. 24, 36, 1997.

Leah Niederstadt is a D.Phil. candidate in social anthropology at Wolfson College, University of Oxford and a graduate student in the Museum Studies Program at the University of Michigan. She is a visiting scholar at the Institute of Ethiopian Studies of Addis Ababa University. Niederstadt has published and lectured on Addis Ababa's contemporary art market and was a contributing author to *Painting Ethiopia: the Life and Work of Qes Adamu Tesfaw* by Raymond A. Silverman (2005).

Fig. 1 Tesfahun Kibru in his studio.
Photograph by Leah
Niederstadt, 2006

Introduction

In 2000 I visited an art exhibition at the Alliance Ethio-Française in Addis Ababa. I remember my surprise at the work of Engdaget Legesse, then known for what he calls "magic pillars": long, narrow pieces of wood painted in abstract designs.[1] I had expected to see what an expatriate friend calls "Two Women" art, which he once advised another *ferengi* (foreigner) to buy "as almost everyone is painting two women. So make sure to get one of those. Sixty-five percent of the paintings…are of two women, carrying baskets, carrying children, making coffee!" His comments were not unfounded. Tamrat Gezahegne, who is featured in this exhibition, has also bemoaned the lack of support for artists experimenting beyond this genre. "When people come to the art, they don't know anything…they want traditional art, people with the coffee, the market, that kind of thing." The struggle to make a living and maintain creativity is one faced by artists worldwide, and it is no different for painters and sculptors working in Ethiopia.

Yet as this exhibition demonstrates, many Ethiopian artists experiment with materials and technique, finding inspiration in the mundane and the unique. This essay focuses on the challenges faced by recent graduates of the Fine Arts School (FAS)[2] and on their desire to create art that is true to their vision and that earns them a living.[3] Life as a full-time studio artist—the aspiration of many FAS graduates—is not easy. *Menor kebad new* (life is difficult), they say. Indeed, life is difficult for many in Ethiopia, but it is uniquely so for them as they face family pressure to succeed, preferably in a career that provides status and income, neither of which art is seen to offer. I draw on numerous conversations with Tamrat Gezahegne and Tesfahun Kibru, the two youngest artists in *Continuity and Change*, and on discussions with other artists, FAS instructors, gallery owners and art buyers, all of whom contribute to Addis Ababa's thriving contemporary art community.

Educating Artists

Whether trained in the traditions of the Ethiopian Orthodox Church,[4] at the FAS or self-taught, present-day Ethiopian artists share an interest in art that began in childhood. For Tesfahun and Tamrat, their desire to create began before school and helped them—for a time—to succeed academically. Tesfahun commented, "When I was in kindergarten…I would draw something on paper. Then the teacher would… ask me to draw the same thing on the backboard. They would say 'Very good!' and the students would clap! …Outside of school, I would see the activities of the city, and I would draw them."

Tamrat's experience was similar:

> When I was a child…for me, it was *yeqelim timhirt* (art education). Education like math, religion, chemistry, it was difficult for me, but making art was comfortable… In school I sometimes made a sketch for the biology teacher of bodies [or] kidneys. …I remember when we were children we made sculptures with *chikka* (mud) and put them on the asphalt in front of the American Embassy.[5] When they were destroyed [by the] cars, we were so happy!

Each experimented with drawing in several mediums on a variety of surfaces, working with *chikka*, and modifying clothing. As a child, Tesfahun made shoes out of the plastic liners found inside metal bottle caps and he now embellishes all of his clothing (fig. 1). As a teenager Tamrat painted his jacket with images of Bruce Lee and Chuck Norris, taking inspiration from the bootleg videos he watched in his neighbourhood. Like Tesfahun, he continues to modify his clothing by changing buttons and adding scraps of fabric (fig. 2). Around the age of eleven Tamrat began constructing the *chikka* sculptures, which evolved beyond those intended for destruction. "One time, ...I made a *chikka* TV...I put glass (a mirror) inside and I went in front of the American Embassy and I put it in a corner and I 'watched' TV because there were people walking and cars passing in the reflection."

When asked how his parents reacted, Tamrat replied, "In my artistic experiences, they did not say anything to me. I remember...a photograph they took and I [copied] it and [placed] it in their bedroom, so they were happy." Tesfahun's parents, too, are supportive:

> After some time, they [became] happy with my work. ...At first, they were thinking about income...but after some time, they began to see I can be an artist and earn money. ...It's not that they do not like art; they do. But it's more about the economy of the country that forces them to ask about the ability to live as an artist.

Many FAS graduates do well in elementary school, when art is in the curriculum. But in secondary school, Tamrat and Tesfahun found their interest in school decreased when art was no longer taught.

> Within the education system, I did not have a good result... My interest was different, it was to learn what I wanted, but I was forced to learn something [else]... If the teacher had extra time or was interested in art, they would teach us but they were not [trained as] art teachers... To be an artist, it is all about training yourself. ...You have to be persistent and struggle. (Tesfahun)

Tamrat said, "I had a good mark for gymnastics, art, and music so I did not fail; these subjects helped me [but] in grade eight, there was no music, art and sport; it was [cut] out." Tamrat remained in school until 1989 when he passed the entrance exams for the FAS; Tesfahun entered in the same class. Although Tamrat built *chikka* sculptures as a child, he chose to major in painting. "The life situation... it [does] not push you to make sculptures. When I was a child, I made these sculptures with *chikka* but when you go to school you find paper and you make [drawings]." When they attended the FAS, painting and graphic design were the most popular concentrations, the former due to a bias toward painting as "real art," and the latter because, as artist Matewos Legesse said, "if you study graphics, first you get variety. You get to learn many different things and then, you also have a good chance to get a job when you finish because you can work for a private business or the government." Mural painting and sculpture were less popular because they were not considered economically viable or "real art", perhaps due to their use as propaganda during the Derg regime (1974-1991).

Tesfahun chose to concentrate in sculpture in part due to his having found a mentor in Bekele Mekonnen, another artist featured in this exhibition. "In the third year, I met Bekele. He was not [then] my teacher but we exchanged ideas and he gave me something important, something to grab on to." For centuries, apprenticeships and mentoring have played key roles in the education of church artists. Fathers often teach their sons to paint, gradually increasing responsibility until they produce work unsupervised (fig. 3).[6] Mentoring plays less of a role in contemporary art education in Ethiopia, and FAS students with mentors greatly value these relationships. While at the FAS, Tamrat had a mentoring relationship with Mezgebu Tessema, a painting instructor.

> [When] I made a sketch, I had to show... Mezgebu. One thing which I never forgot is that he looked [at] that sketch and [said], 'the sketch by this size, it is very nice. But when you convert it to [canvas], this space will be [too] big, so what will you do?' ...That education has helped me to see spaces and forms and shapes. How to make visual music inside [the canvas] with different forms.

Fig. 2   Tamrat Gezahegne in his studio, standing in front of recent paintings. Photograph by Leah Niederstadt, 2006

I can see where I could have gone then with my art. …I do not believe in the idea of 'graduated' or 'not graduated' when it comes to being an artist. I just want to see the result of someone's work. I do not care about their qualifications. Unless they are able to show that they learned there, for me, it means nothing.

Life as a Full-Time Studio Artist

Following graduation, most artists seek employment as graphic designers or establish studios. Since 2001, the number of these studios, which also serve as galleries, has increased significantly. Like Asni Gallery, the Goethe Institute and several new restaurants-cum-galleries, these artist-run studios provide space for creating and exhibiting art and for engaging in discussion with other artists,[7] most of whom are men. Social norms limit the number of women who apply to the FAS and restrict their career choices upon graduation. Young female artists face family pressure to marry and have children; and those that do usually stop working as artists, although Mihret Dawit is an exception. As Tamrat once commented, "they just disappear." As of 2006, among full-time studio artists in Addis, very few are women. Each year, three to five female students are typically admitted to the FAS[8] but as Tadesse Mesfin, an artist in this exhibition, once commented, "It is difficult for them; they are not free to leave their houses. The boys, they are free… to explore and to visit studios and exhibitions. But the girls, they must stay in the house so they do not have access [to the art world]." Although they occasionally mount group exhibitions, few women artists actively participate in the art community, although noted exceptions include Desta Hagos, Martha Mengistu, Kerima Ahmed and Bisrat Shibabaw. Works by Bisrat and Desta are included in this exhibition. In the last three years, however, several more young women have begun exhibiting, which bodes well for the future of Addis Ababa's art community and the society in general.

Young women are not alone in facing pressure to pursue other careers. Their male peers express frustration with the lack of familial and public understanding of or support for art. "When you are out in the neighbourhood, there is negative thinking about creative works, like weaving,

Fig. 3   Two generations of church painters: *Haleqa* Berhane Gebre Iyasus and his son Abraham Berhane. Photograph by Leah Niederstadt, 2005

The incorporation of the FAS into Addis Ababa University in 2000 changed the admission requirements. While students previously were chosen for their artistic ability, they now must gain a minimum point result on their secondary school exams. Tamrat, Tesfahun and many other recent graduates would not be admitted to the FAS under this new policy. "There are a lot of students who cannot enter because of the point system. They have the ability; they can do the work, but there are even students who had to stop [school] because of this." (Tesfahun) Although Tamrat and Tesfahun feel that their experiences at the FAS helped them to grow as artists, both believe that they learned the most from their conversations with other students and their instructors. Tesfahun commented:

It was a chance for me to meet other people, to talk to them and that was good. I could get information there. The bad thing was that we only learned what they wanted to teach us, which was realistic painting. Students were not given enough opportunity to contribute their ideas. There were good things, it was not all bad; but now when I think about it, I realize that if there had not been [certain] pressures from the teachers, pottery, art. I do not know why it became like that… What is the problem that people do not have a good interpretation (opinion) for this work but they have a good interpretation for doctors?" (Tamrat) FAS graduates who choose to work as artists face several further challenges. A very few, such as Fikru Gebre Mariam, focus on exhibiting abroad, made possible by their financial resources and ability to network. Most young artists only exhibit in Ethiopia although some, including Debebe Tesfaye, Solomon Asfaw, Engdaget Legesse, Mulugeta Gebrekidane and Matewos Legesse, regularly exhibit at home and abroad. A few establish studios alone, but many prefer to work collectively, like Debebe and Solomon, who founded Saron Studio. Habesha Art Studio is another well-known group studio, among the first to be founded post-Derg. After deciding how best to live and work, young artists must then negotiate the shifting alliances and personality conflicts that develop within studios and among their peer group; find exhibition space and materials; and cultivate gallery owners and clients. In their search for materials, many young artists, including Elias Sime, whose work is in this exhibition, utilize found objects, purposely incorporating the detritus of daily life into their work.

Tamrat and Tesfahun chose to work together after graduation. Tesfahun said their friendship "gave us the strength to continue and to experiment. It helped us to collaborate." They began by creating what they call "souvenir works" to sell to tourist shops for start-up capital. Tamrat remembered, "With that money, we paid for the rent [for a studio] and we got the chance to experiment, work and exhibit." Tamrat also sold portrait sketches while sitting in cafés and restaurants. In 2003, along with Mulugeta Kassa, Dawit Geresu, Asnake Tegegn and Leikun Nawsenay, they founded New Art Space Studio near Ras Makonnen Bridge in the Piazza neighbourhood. Located in the basement of an old house, the large high-ceilinged space enabled them to experiment further. Tamrat recalled, "With the big studio I started making big works…because when I was in the little studio, I was making little paintings." In February 2006 some of these large-scale paintings were exhibited in Asni Gallery; all but one sold.

Although appreciative of artistic or financial success when it arrives, young artists must then face the challenges it generates, as maintaining artistic creativity and integrity is a struggle when *menor kebad new* (life is difficult). Family pressure to generate income is significant and young artists explore various solutions. Some work part-time in graphic design or regularly produce "souvenir works" as Tamrat and Tesfahun once did. Others are believed to track exhibitions to identify and then emulate the type of work that sells, although few people will openly discuss the practice. One artist, who asked to remain anonymous, calls them "What's Up Artists," labelled for the Addis Ababa entertainment guide that lists upcoming exhibitions. He said, "when I see our work, it seems like [we are] always copying from each other." In a similar manner, an expatriate living in Addis once warned me to confirm that the painting I planned to buy was not a copy.[9] Many encourage artists to experiment and find their own styles, but one gallery owner anonymously offered a practical solution:

> If you have an exhibition, show your own work, your own creative idea. Then, if you copy something, you can sell it in a different way, at a different time. …But at an exhibition? It is just stupid. The people who go to the exhibitions…They know about art in Addis…They can tell if someone is copying and if someone is doing his own creative idea.

Art as business, as a money-making endeavour, challenges young artists and gallery owners who want to show a range of artworks, but cannot afford to exhibit work they cannot sell. The aforementioned gallery owner clarified the situation faced by artists who work outside of the "What's Up" or "Two Women" genre. "Many people who come to Ethiopia…want to buy something that reminds them of Ethiopia, something that is 'Ethiopian'[10] and to their mind, modern is not Ethiopia. I mean, they do not want modern, abstract art." Tamrat agreed:

> If you want to sell, you have to make touristic[11] [sic] paintings. [But] when you make touristic paintings, you will not be happy. Your aim will be to get money, not to go deep (experiment) in art… The souvenir works helped us to pay for our rent and to buy some materials

and we made only experimental works. And when we became in love with these experimental works, we hated the souvenir works.

After his 2000 exhibition, Engdaget Legesse stopped making "magic pillars", even when he struggled financially:

I used to do it because the work was genuine. Now I can sell them. People want to buy them, but I cannot even try. …Thinking about money and painting together, I cannot do it. …If I did the magic pillars…for the sake of solving my [financial] problem, it would be great… but I cannot do it.

Perhaps, as artists like Engdaget, Tamrat and Tesfahun are increasingly lauded by critics and collectors, Ethiopia's contemporary art market will allow more room for experimental or modern art. Certainly some, such as Elias Sime, rarely, if ever, consider producing art for the market. Others, however, find the issue less problematic or at various stages of their careers are forced by their financial circumstances to create work in several genres.

Plans for the Future

In the past few years, young Ethiopian artists have begun travelling abroad for exhibitions and residency programs. Some, like painter Teferi Gizachew, have made multiple trips. A few left and failed to return, making it more difficult for others to obtain the visas needed for travel. Still others have travelled once or twice and are seeking further opportunities, as the options for graduate arts education in Ethiopia are non-existent. In addition, although active, the Addis Ababa arts community is somewhat insular; and even with the advent of the Internet, access to information about the arts, such as exhibition catalogues, is limited. Almost all artists I know, regardless of their ages, want greater public and government support for the arts and are attempting to engender such change. Tamrat and Tesfahun used to hold discussions in their studio, inviting their peers, former instructors and others interested in the arts, but they found "it is very difficult to understand each other…to share ideas… Many

times, we tried to have discussions, but it did not work." (Tesfahun)

The conflicts arising from these discussions varied, but attempts to discuss the challenges of living as an artist and of emulation generated controversy due to the sensitivity of the topic and a near universal aversion to admitting publicly to producing for the market, however defined, for fear of being identified as someone who is not a "real" artist. Yet most gallery owners, art buyers and artists are aware of these challenges and comment on them, often in ways that support the debatable label of "real artist." Others see these challenges as a non-issue. For example, I have often been asked to recommend artists who do reproductions, because "I saw this work at an exhibit and I really liked it, but it was already marked as sold." Many recognize that the Addis Ababa art market, like others worldwide, constantly alters as trends change, meaning at one time or another, most artists will struggle with how best to make a living while holding onto their creative vision.

For Tamrat and Tesfahun, the solution is constant experimentation and searching for inspiration in all aspects of life.

You get the ideas from what you see. There are children, people, different kinds of characters, and illnesses like leprosy. When I see people with leprosy, I am looking at it from the sculptural point of view…It gives me inspiration. …People talk about things being ugly [and] it is difficult for me to talk with them because for me…when I see everything…there is a beautiful shape, there are lines. (Tamrat) (fig.4)

Both Tamrat and Tesfahun are keenly concerned with the future of the arts in Ethiopia and are interested in improving the status quo however best they can. When asked about his wish for the future, Tesfahun replied:

It is very difficult to say how the future would look, but my wish is for the art movement to move away a little from the business and to concentrate more on the art. …It is not something a person can do alone…if you have more connections

Fig. 4 Tamrat Gezahegne
Man with Leprosy, 2006
Colored pen and marker on paper
11 x 8 1/2 in. (27.9 x 21.6 cm.)
Collection of the artist.
Photography courtesy
of Leah Niederstadt

within the art [and performance] world… there will be sharing, and when that happens, we will understand each other.

Given their educational experiences, many young artists are interested in teaching art and quite a few already do so informally on temporary projects or more formally in schools. Although interested in teaching, Tesfahun clarified what that meant for him. "When I teach, I do not want students to follow me… I do not want to put pressure on the students to become an 'artist.' I just want them to find themselves in their own way." Tamrat already considers himself a teacher:

Maybe what I am doing, my life by itself, it is teaching. What I am putting on my body, on my clothes…[it is] like painting on myself, like putting an installation on myself [because] it gives me inspiration and at the same time, it gives ideas for others and it creates discussion. So like that, indirectly I am teaching.

Conclusion

Since graduation from the FAS, Tamrat and Tesfahun have continuously experimented with their art and with their lives as young Ethiopian artists. They move from one medium or technique to another rather than reproducing what sells, a criticism often levelled at young artists. Tamrat and Tesfahun pursue change not from a lack of financial or critical artistic success, but from a desire to engage with new ideas and resources, with the people they encounter and the world in which they live. In doing so, they produce works that are increasingly sought after by collectors, even when their size and media are not yet favoured by most *ferengi* (foreign) buyers. They struggle with the challenges that face all young artists in Addis Ababa, utilizing materials at hand, sharing studio and living space, and finding inspiration in the diversity for which Ethiopia is famed. As Tesfahun recently said, "Art should be how I live. It should be just like life. It should not be limited by anything. … My hope is just to be completely living in art. …All things in life give me inspiration and I do not know where it will take me but I want to keep it like that!" For those of us who value Ethiopia's traditions of creativity in all their myriad forms, the lives of the country's youngest artists are worth further examination and study. Among them are the mature artists of the future and the teachers and mentors of the next generation.

---

1 Engdaget's "magic pillars" draw on images associated with magic or healing scrolls. For more on the scrolls, see Jacque Mercier's *Ethiopian Magic Scrolls* (1979) or *Art That Heals: the Image as Medicine in Ethiopia* (1997). Elisabeth Biasio has also written about contemporary artists who find inspiration in the scrolls. "Magic Scrolls in Modern Ethiopian Painting," *Africana Bulletin* 52 (Warsaw University, Warsaw, Polland, 2004), 31-42.

2 The FAS was renamed the School of Fine Arts and Design when it became part of Addis Ababa University in 2000. In this essay, FAS will be used, as this is how all of the artists with whom I work refer to the school.

3 This essay relies on ongoing research among artists, gallery owners and art patrons in Ethiopia. I thank all of them, too numerable to be listed here, for sharing their time, thoughts, hopes and, of course, their art.

4 For more on art education in the Ethiopian Orthodox Church, see *Ethiopia: Traditions of Creativity* (1999), edited by Raymond Silverman, especially the introduction and essay on *Qes* Adamu Tesfaw and the essay co-written with Girma Fisseha. Also see Silverman's *Painting Ethiopia: The Life and Work of Qes Adamu Tesfaw* (2005).

5 Tamrat's family lives in Shiromeda, a neighbourhood near the American Embassy in Addis Ababa. Known for its textile market, Shiromeda is home to many *shemanay* (weavers). Gezahegne Gero, Tamrat's father, is a *shemanay* and is Dorze, an ethnic group long recognized for producing skilled weavers. Tamrat credits his interest in artwork as coming from his father, even though he initially wanted Tamrat to focus on academic studies.

6 Church painters often come from generations of the same family. *Qes* Adamu Tesfaw, the artist featured in Raymond Silverman's aforementioned book, studied with his godfather *Ato* Yohannis Tesemma, while his uncle *Aleqa* Kassa Getahun was a well-known painter in Gojjam. The practice of passing artistic traditions from one generation to the next continues today in Aksum where several church artists are training their children, including their daughters, to paint.

7 Given the cost of housing and business space in Addis Ababa, most young artists also live in their studios.

8 According to Léo Lefort, a former FAS lecturer, 572 students graduated from the FAS between 1957 and 1997 and 74 of these graduates were women. Thus, during the first forty years of the school's existence, 13 percent of FAS graduates were women.

9 In this instance, a relative had purchased a painting from a gallery and returned several months later to see an exact reproduction of the work for sale. When he complained, he was given the second, duplicate work for free.

10 Although the question of what is or is not "Ethiopian" art or an "Ethiopian" artist is worth exploring, I am unable to do so within this essay.

11 "Touristic paintings" refers to the "Two Woman" genre, i.e., art produced for sale in galleries but judged to be derivative or an obvious copy. "Souvenir works", which Tamrat and Tesfahun have both produced, refers to paintings of scenes of daily life and historical figures, usually produced on *qoda* (leather hide) and sold in tourist shops and at the Mercato, Addis Ababa's central market area.

Agegnehu Engida

Born in the Gondar Administrative Region in 1905, Agegnehu Engida was among the first Ethiopian artists to attend a foreign art academy. He studied at the Ecole des Beaux-Arts in Paris from 1926 to 1933. After returning to Addis Ababa, he had several exhibitions and received commissions for military uniforms and currency designs for the government, church mural paintings and portraits. Ladislas Fargo met the artist in Addis Ababa in 1930. He described Agegnehu as a disciple of the impressionists and admired his landscapes and "pictures of native life" more than the portraits for which he was most noted. According to Fargo, upon Agegnehu's return from Paris he was shunned by both his fellow Ethiopians and the European community in Addis Ababa because of the Swiss girlfriend who accompanied him. Agegnehu fled with the young woman to the southern province of Arusi. Unhappy, she contacted her father, who took her back to Switzerland. When Farago visited Agegnehu at his home in Addis Ababa, the artist was married to a woman whom Farago called "a typical Amharic beauty" and "the most beautiful woman I met in Abyssinia."[1]

In 1941 Agegnehu was appointed assistant director of the newly established Department of Fine Arts in the Ministry of Education and Fine Arts. Around the same time he set up an informal art school, a forerunner of the Fine Arts School founded in 1957/58 by Ale Felege Selam Heruy. Agegnehu Engida died in Addis Ababa in 1950.

Two of Agegnehu's portraits survive in the collection of the National Museum of Ethiopia, a self portrait from 1944 and a portrait of Aster Mengesha, a famous beauty of the day. Unfortunately, the latter needs conservation and is not exhibited at the museum. Both paintings reveal Agegnehu's talent for capturing a realistic likeness and suggesting personality or mood. In his self portrait the artist presents himself in European-style business clothes and with well-trimmed moustache and goatee. Dapper in a dark blue velvet beret and wire rimmed spectacles, he gazes confidently but with a bemused expression at the viewer.

1   Ladislas Fargo, *Abyssinia on the Eve* (New York: G. P. Putnam's Sons, 1935), 112, 114

Agegnehu Engida, 1905-1950, *Self Portrait*, 1944, oil on canvas
19 7/8 x 15 in. (50.5 x 38.1 cm.), collection of the National Museum of Ethiopia

Afewerk Tekle was born in Ankober in Shoa Province in 1932. Because of his abilities in mathematics and draftsmanship, Haile Selassie sent Afewerk to London to study mining engineering in 1947. The Emperor soon granted permission for Afewerk to transfer to London's Central School of Arts and Crafts. Subsequently, Afewerk attended the Slade School of Fine Art at the University of London. While studying in England he made several artistic pilgrimages to the European continent.

Afewerk held his first solo exhibition in Addis Ababa in 1954. Soon thereafter he returned to Europe, where he traveled on the continent for two years. Afewerk was profoundly influenced by his studies in Europe, and throughout his career has moved fluidly between figural and abstract imagery based on his interpretations of Western artistic styles. His love for his Ethiopian heritage is expressed in the subject matter rather than the style of his paintings and sculptures. Throughout his career, Afewerk has been sufficiently flexible in his choice of themes to benefit from the patronage of three successive regimes, the imperial government of Haile Selassie (overthrown in 1974), the Derg regime of Mengistu Haile Mariam (1974-1991) and the present government of Prime Minister Meles Zenawi (1995 to present).

Afewerk has won numerous national and international awards including the Prix de Rome in 1955. He was the first recipient of the Haile Selassie I Prize Trust Award in 1964 "for his outstanding drawings, paintings, landscapes, and portraits which eloquently express his particular world environment, and for his contribution in being among the first to introduce contemporary techniques to Ethiopian subject matter and content."[2] Afwerk has exhibited his work and lectured in various countries of Africa, Europe, the Middle East and in the United States. In 1981 his *Self Portrait* was the first by an artist from the African continent to be included in the permanent collection of the Uffizi Gallery in Florence.

Afewerk's first commission in Addis Ababa was for murals and mosaics at St. George's Cathedral, a project that occupied him for three and a half years. During the same period he completed a series of stained glass windows of Ethiopian warrior heroes for the military academy in Harar and a bronze equestrian monument to Ras Makonnen, father of Emperor Haile Sellassie, also in Harar. In 1959 Afewerk received the commission to design a stained glass window for the Africa Hall of the United Nations Economic Commission for Africa in Addis Ababa. The resulting composition, *The Struggle and Aspiration of the African People*, incorporates pan-African themes in a definitive statement against colonialism. The monumental composition, measuring 150 square meters, is among his best-known works.

2   Richard Pankhurst, *Afewerk Tekle* (Àddis Ababa: Artistic Printers of Ethiopia, 1987), 43

Afewerk made his first trip to the Soviet Union in 1964 and returned with a new interest in Western classical ballet. *Homage to Russian Ballet*,[3] painted in 1968, is related in style to his stained glass window designs for the Military Academy in Harar and, especially, for Africa Hall in Addis Ababa. In the latter stained glass composition, Afewerk introduced a bold network of curved and straight black lines that correspond neither to individual pieces of glass nor to the details of the figural composition. Rather, the black lines constitute an independent compositional device, overlaying an abstract linear pattern onto a traditional figural composition.

Afewerk designed his imposing house, studio and gallery in 1959 and completed construction over the course of fifteen years. Known as Villa Alpha, the structure is modeled on historic Ethiopian stone architecture in ancient Aksum and medieval Gondar in the north and the walled city of Harar in the east. Although Afewerk is not associated with the School of Fine Arts in Addis Ababa and never taught or took apprentices, his national and international recognition, awards and prominent commissions and financial success have made him a role model for many Ethiopian artists.

3   Permission was not granted by the artist to reproduce the painting. Afewerk Tekle, born 1932 *Homage to Russian Ballet*, 1968 Oil on canvas, 67 x 48 1/4 in. (170.2 x 122.6 cm.) Smithsonian Institution, National Museum of African Art, gift of Joseph and Patricia Brumit, 2004-7-64

Born in the Shoa administrative district in 1924, Ale Felege Selam Heruy grew up around a grandfather and uncle who were well known church painters, but was never interested in apprenticing with his relatives. Instead, he learned the canons of church painting from observing their work and taught himself to draw and paint. Eventually he graduated with distinction from the Addis Ababa Technical School and was selected by the Emperor for the opportunity to study abroad. He spent five years at the School of the Art Institute of Chicago studying studio art and art education and completing his degree in 1954. After traveling for three months in France and Italy, he returned to Addis Ababa where he recruited local high school students to take art classes at his home. The enthusiasm of his students strengthened Ale Felege's resolve to establish a formal school for the fine arts in Addis Ababa. With the support of Emperor Haile Selassie, the Addis Ababa School of Fine Arts was founded in 1957/58 with Ale Felege as its first director. *Ato* Ale (Mr. Ale), as his former students and friends call him, served as director of the school until 1975. He is now retired and living in Nazret, Ethiopia, where he remains active as a painter and pursues his hobby of fishing in local rivers and lakes.

Ale Felege is recognized as a landscape and portrait painter. In addition, although he did not receive the traditional training of a church artist, he has painted murals in several important churches including Trinity Cathedral and the churches of St. Mary and St. Raguel in Addis Ababa. He painted an extensive cycle of murals for the large church of St. Mary in Nazret, a project that occupied him for three years. In 2006 he painted the monumental cupola of the Dabra Ghenet Medhanialem Ethiopian Orthodox Church in Temple Hill, Maryland.

Although Ale Felege's academic training in Chicago prepared him to paint representational imagery using chiaroscuro and other Western techniques (fig. 1), he often employs a style that is more indebted to that of Ethiopian church painting with simplified flattened forms and broad areas of bright, clear color, as seen in his serene rendering of a familiar landscape vista from 1974/75.

Fig. 1 Ale Felege Selam Heruy, born 1924
Portrait of Dr. Otto, 1962
Oil on canvas
31 3/16 x 23 7/8 in. (79.2 x 60.7 cm.)
Collection of the artist

Ale Felege Selam Heruy, born 1924, *Untitled*, 1974-75, oil on board
14 x 20 in. (35.6 x 50.8 cm.), on loan from Eshetu Tiruneh

Skunder Boghossian was born in Addis Ababa in 1937 and died in Washington, D.C. in 2003.[4] He studied art informally at Tafari Makonnen secondary school and with Stanislas Chojnacki, a historian of Ethiopian art and watercolorist, who was then librarian at the University College of Addis Ababa. In 1955 Skunder won second prize at an art exhibition held as part of Haile Selassie's Jubilee Anniversary Celebration. As a result he was awarded an imperial scholarship to study in London. He attended St. Martin's School, the Central School and the Slade School of Fine Art in London before moving to Paris in 1957. There he studied at the Ecole nationale supérieure de beaux-arts and the Académie de la Grande Chaumière. However, Skunder spent most of his time in cafés and jazz clubs, museums and artists' studios, reveling in the intellectual and artistic fervor of Paris. Through his exposure to philosophers and writers such as Cheikh Anta Diop, Aimé Césaire and Leopold Senghor and artists such as André Breton, Roberto Matta, Wifredo Lam and Gerard Sokoto, he explored the theories of Negritude, Pan-Africanism and Surrealism. He studied traditional African art and systems of thought through his friendship with Madeleine Rousseau, an art historian and collector. Skunder's compositions from the Paris years, with their kaleidoscopic layering of form, meaning, color and design, reflect his interest in pan-African themes as well as his Ethiopian heritage. Skunder returned to Addis Ababa in 1966 and joined the faculty at the Addis Ababa School of Fine Arts. Although he taught in Ethiopia for only three years, Skunder's impact was lasting. A number of Ethiopian students traveled to the United States to study with him during his long career as a professor at Howard University in Washington, D.C. (1971–2001). Early in his career Skunder's work entered the collections of the Musée d'Art moderne de la ville de Paris and the Museum of Modern Art in New York. His work has been widely exhibited in Africa, Europe and the Americas and is included in numerous museum and private collections.

Night Flight of Dread and Delight, painted in Paris in 1964, suggests the enchantment of dreams and the menace of nightmares. The midnight sky explodes with jewel-like stars and orbs, biomorphic forms, a winged spirit and an ascendant owl. Intrigued by the work of surrealist artists in Paris, Skunder drew on age-old Ethiopian and West African stories about powerful visions, supernatural forces and mystical transformations. At the time he was reading the novels of Nigerian writer Amos Tutuola, which are filled with imagery of spirits and nightmarish metamorphoses.[5]

The End of the Beginning, 1972, painted soon after Skunder's arrival at Howard University, portrays a winged being with massive horns and hollow peering eyes, a menacing reptile and two birds against the backdrop of a turbulent landscape infused with shades of red that suggest sunset, fire, even blood. Skunder's paintings at this time dealt with themes of political oppression, violence and destruction, as in the 1972 painting *DMZ* (for demilitarized zone) in the collection of Howard University Museum, which may relate to the Vietnam War.

Acha Debela recalls that Skunder traveled throughout Africa in the mid 1970s with Ghanaian art historian Kojo Fosu to organize an exhibition of contemporary African art for Howard University. While in Africa, Skunder collected ideas and materials with which he would experiment later in works like *Time Cycle III*. This somber, heraldic composition has a visual impact far more monumental than its physical dimensions would suggest. It is fashioned from bark collected by the artist in Uganda, combined with collage elements and a vertical column of sand along the right border. The symmetrical geometry of the composition combined with evocative motifs such as the heraldic lion contribute to a powerful sense of the sacred.

4   The artist's name was Eskunder (Alexander) Boghossian, but he used the shortened form of the name, Skunder.
5   Solomon Deressa discusses the influence of Tutuola on the artist in "Skunder in Context," *Ethiopian BIR Business and Industry Report*, vol. 3, no. 1, January/February 1997, 27.

Skunder Boghossian, 1937-2003, *Night Flight of Dread and Delight*, 1964, oil on canvas with collage
56 5/8 x 5 ft. 2 5/8 in. (143.8 x 159.1 cm.), North Carolina Museum of Art, Raleigh
Purchased with funds from the North Carolina Art Society (Robert F. Phifer Bequest), 98.6

Skunder Boghossian, 1937-2003, *The End of the Beginning*, 1972-1973, oil on canvas
48 1/4 in. x 67 in. (122.6 x 170.2 cm.), museum purchase, 91-18-2
Photograph by Franko Khoury, National Museum of African Art, Smithsonian Institution

Skunder Boghossian, 1937-2003, *Time Cycle III*, 1981, embossed bark and sand with collage on board
48 x 47 7/8 in. (121.9 x 121.6 cm.), museum purchase, funds provided by the Caroline J. and James G. Richardson
Art Acquisition Endowment, and the Charles P. and Caroline Ireland Foundation, collection of the Samuel P. Harn Museum of Art, 2006.3

Gebre Kristos Desta was born in Harar, Ethiopia in 1932 and completed his elementary education there. He graduated from the elite General Wingate High School in Addis Ababa and attended University College of Addis Ababa to study agricultural science at the insistence of his family. After his second year at college, he determined to pursue his goal of becoming a professional artist and in 1957 won a scholarship to study art at the Werkschule für Bildende Künste und Gestaltung in Cologne, Germany. After graduating at the top of his class in 1961, Gebre Kristos remained in Europe for a year, working in his private studio in Cologne and traveling widely on the continent. Shortly after his return to Addis Ababa in 1962, he joined the faculty of the Fine Arts School where he taught until 1978. When Gebre Kristos held his first solo exhibition in Addis Ababa in 1963 he was sharply criticized for abandoning Ethiopian representational traditions to embrace European-inspired abstraction. Gebre Kristos emerged as an eloquent champion of expressionistic and abstract art and encouraged his students to experiment with contemporary styles and mediums.

A sculptor and poet as well a painter, he was also an unwavering advocate of interdisciplinary experimentation. As such he was a driving force during the "Addis Spring," the florescence of visual, literary and performing arts in Addis Ababa in the 1960s. Although Gebre Kristos remained in Addis Ababa after the overthrow of Haile Selassie, he eventually succumbed to mounting pressures from the Derg regime and sought asylum outside Ethiopia. He arrived in the United States in 1980, finding refuge in Lawton, Oklahoma. He held a one-man show in Oklahoma City before his untimely death in 1981.

Gebre Kristos was recipient of many honors, including the Haile Sellassie I Prize Trust Award for the Fine Arts in 1965. During his lifetime his work was widely exhibited in Africa, Europe and North America as well as in India. Since 1991, Gebre Kristos' accomplishments as an artist and poet and his profound impact as a teacher have been celebrated and honored in Ethiopia. In 2006 the German Cultural Institute named its Goethe Institute building in Addis Ababa the Gebrekristos Desta Center, opening the facility with an exhibition of Gebre Kristos' paintings, and collaborating with the Institute for Ethiopian Studies of Addis Ababa University to publish a book on his art and one on his poetry.

Although his work is often characterized as a personal response to German expressionism or abstract expressionism, Gebre Kristos' oeuvre falls into several distinctive stylistic and thematic groupings. These include portraits; figural compositions with skeletal forms and others with mummy-like wrapped forms; brilliantly colored, exuberant landscapes and still lifes; experimental abstract collages and assemblages; and abstract paintings with dominant circular motifs and radiating straight lines. *Organic* (1965) is among the abstract compositions of circles to which the artist referred when he commented: "The circle is infinite, unending. It symbolizes the hemisphere and heavenly bodies. It is in line with the search for a solution in life, when it frequently happens that one may believe he has reached the optimum solution only to find, since art is life itself, that the search must continue, a perfect solution remains forever elusive."[6] An intaglio print titled *Vergessen* (To Forget), dated 1959, and a related untitled painting from 1966 incorporate prominent circles and energetic radiating diagonal lines. Although abstract, the horizontal composition of the painting hints at the setting sun and winter-bare branches and resonates with the artist's more representational landscape and still life paintings. During the Derg regime, Gebre Kristos, like all faculty and students at the Fine Arts School, was called upon to design posters, banners and other ephemera for the Marxist government. *Struggle for Victory* (1977) is the preliminary design for a poster advertising a play of the same name by Denekew Asaye to be performed at the Addis Ababa Municipality Culture Hall.

6   David Talbot, "The Art of Gabra Kristos Desta: Press Comment on a recent Exhibition: Artist Gabra Kristos X-Rayed," *Ethiopia Observer*, vol. 9, no. 4, 1966, 285.

Gebre Kristos Desta, 1932-1981, *Organic*, 1969, oil on board
46 1/4 x 38 1/8 in. (117.5 x 96.8 cm.), collection of Mesfin Gebreyes Oda, Addis Ababa

Gebre Kristos Desta, 1932-1981, *Untitled*, 1966, oil on canvas
19 x 38 1/2 in. (48.3 x 97.8 cm.), collection of Mesfin Gebreyes Oda, Addis Ababa

Gebre Kristos Desta, 1932-1981, *Vergessen* (To Forget), 1959, intaglio print
23 x 13 1/2 in. (58.4 x 34.3 cm.), collection of Mesfin Gebreyes Oda, Addis Ababa

Gebre Kristos Desta, 1932-1981, Design for theater poster for *Struggle for Victory*, 1977, ink and watercolor on paper
25 x 16 in. (63.5 x 40.6 cm.), collection of Mesfin Gebreyes Oda, Addis Ababa

Desta Hagos

Desta Hagos was born in Adwa in the Tigray region of northern Ethiopia in 1952. She moved to Addis Ababa at age nine to attend boarding school and later attended the prestigious Empress Menen High School, a school for girls. When she received her diploma from the Addis Ababa Fine Arts School in 1969, Desta's graduation exhibition was the first solo show by a woman artist in Ethiopia. She subsequently received a BFA from California Lutheran University in 1973. When Desta and her husband Yohannes returned to Ethiopia in 1974/75 they found the country in turmoil. Yohannes fled for his life but Desta was not allowed to leave the country. She remained behind in Addis Ababa to give birth two months later to a daughter, whom she raised alone. In 1976 Desta began working for the Ethiopian Tourist Organization in the Public Relations Office. Ten years later she transferred to the Ethiopian Tourist Trading Enterprise, where she served as Head of the Artistic Activities Department. In 2002 she retired from public service to devote herself full time to her art. Much of her work is concerned with the daily lives and emotional struggles of women, although she also paints flower still lifes, landscapes and abstract compositions that reveal the enduring influence of her teacher, mentor and friend, Gebre Kristos Desta. Desta Hagos' work has been exhibited in Ethiopia, the United States, Canada and Denmark. She was the first woman artist to be represented in the collection of the National Museum of Ethiopia.

While a student at the Fine Arts School, Desta shared a studio with four male artists at the Creative Arts Center of Addis Ababa University, a venue for exhibitions, theatrical productions, musical and dance performances and poetry readings. Desta often attended gatherings of writers there, including painter/poet Gebre Kristos Desta, art critic/poet Solomon Deressa, poets Mengistu Lemma and Tsegaye Gebre Medhin, and journalist Be'alu Girma, who later was killed by the Derg. She was friends with prominent actors Debebe Eshehtu and Wogayehu Negatu, and was persuaded by them and Mengistu Lemma to play the female lead in a Chekhov play translated into Amharic by Mengistu (she does not now remember which play it was). Leaving aside acting to concentrate on her art, Desta continued to be an enthusiastic member of the audience for performances at the Center and other venues. In *The Stage* (1969) she captures the energy, movement, creativity and imagination of theatrical productions during the "Addis Spring." Desta says that the painting came from her imagination and her general impressions of the theater rather than from a particular stage production. She wanted to convey that the audience is part of the drama, that life itself is a play in which all of us are acting. Indeed, she asks, who is *watching* the play?

Desta Hagos, born 1952, *The Stage*, 1969, oil and collage on board, 33 x 42 7/8 in. (83.8 x 108.9 cm.), collection of Desta Hagos

Born in Addis Ababa in 1952, Lulseged Retta loved to draw from an early age and won numerous prizes for art projects in elementary school. He attended Tafari Makonnen High School and earned his diploma from the Addis Ababa Fine Arts School in 1977. In 1975 the government had proclaimed the Development through Cooperation Campaign (the *zamacha*), which involved sending thousands of high school and university students across the country to help implement land reform in rural areas.[7] After graduating from the art school, Lulseged passed an examination that qualified him for alternate national service in Addis Ababa at the Hager Fikir Theater, where he worked for two years designing posters and stage sets. He was then awarded a scholarship to the Academy of Fine Arts in Leningrad, where he received an MFA with an emphasis on graphic arts in 1987. Back in Addis Ababa, Lulseged had his first solo show at the Alliance Ethio-Française in 1988. For nine years he worked as head graphic designer for the Ethiopian Tourist Trading Enterprise (ETTE), for which he designed a series of posters portraying scenes of daily life in Ethiopia. Although Lulseged left the ETTE in 1996, his popular posters are still sold and widely displayed in residences, offices and commercial establishments. Since 1996, Lulseged has worked as an independent artist and lives from the sale of his paintings. His work has been exhibited in Africa, Europe, Asia and the United States and is represented in private and institutional collections in Africa, Europe and the United States.

Lulseged's *Self Portrait* (1982), painted for a course on portraiture at the Academy in Leningrad, resembles photographs of the young artist at the time. Rail thin, he wore an exuberant Afro and sometimes donned traditional Ethiopian attire of hand-woven white cotton trimmed in scarlet. In this watercolor likeness, his eyes are downcast, his expression introspective. Although it is hard to imagine the gregarious artist as a shy, homesick youth, he speaks today of how lonely and isolated he felt during his first months in the Soviet Union.

While working for the ETTE, Lulseged pursued research on traditional illustrated manuscripts and church mural paintings, which provided inspiration for his graphic designs. His interest in historical art and architecture is evident in the watercolor on parchment titled *Day of Lalibela*. This small composition is the original design for a large mural painted by Lulseged for the Roha Hotel in Lalibela in 1993. The mural celebrates the famous rock-cut churches of Lalibela, the design and execution of which are attributed by legend to the medieval architect and king Lalibela, together with the angels who assisted him to accomplish the gargantuan task of carving monumental buildings from solid bedrock. Near the top left of the design is the seated figure of Lalibela and near the lower right is the cruciform church of St. George, arguably the best-known of the Lalibela churches. In the center of the composition a group of priests displays the veiled *tabot*, a replica of the Ark of the Covenant found in the holy of holies of every Ethiopian Orthodox church and brought out for certain religious festivals.

Gebre Kristos Desta is remembered by his students as a great teacher; a patient and supportive mentor; a brilliant artist and poet; and an elegant and charming man. For *Jazz Night (Tribute to Gebre Kristos Desta)*, painted in 1993, Lulseged chose to imitate the style of his revered teacher and friend, whose approach to composition and color he finds unparalleled. Lulseged listened to jazz and blues while painting this tribute, borrowing Gebre Kristos' vibrant and expressionistic color, repeating circles and bold black lines to suggest a head, mouth, trumpet, hands, drum and drumsticks. *Jazz Night* is a paean to the explosion of creativity and the synergy of the arts in Addis Ababa in the 1960s.

7   Harold G. Marcus, *A History of Ethiopia* (Berkeley: University of California Press, 1994), 192.

Lulseged Retta, born 1952, *Self Portrait*, 1982, watercolor on paper
15 5/8 x 13 1/4 in. (39.7 x 33.7 cm.), collection of the artist

Lulseged Retta, born 1952, *Day of Lalibela*, 1993, watercolor on parchment
8 3/4 x 22 in. (22.2 x 55.9 cm.), collection of the artist

Lulseged Retta, born 1952, *Jazz Night (Tribute to Gebre Kristos Desta)*, 1993, acrylic on cotton cloth on board
59 1/4 x 29 3/4 in. (150.5 x 75.6 cm.), collection of the artist

Yohannes Gedamu

Born in Addis Ababa in 1947, Yohannes attended the Addis Ababa Fine Arts School and graduated in 1967. From 1965-67 he also worked as a part-time designer and scenery artist for the Ethiopian Television Service, and from 1967-69 taught art at a high school in Gondar, Ethiopia. He worked for two years as a graphic designer in Addis Ababa before establishing the Rainbow Art Agency and Gallery, which he ran as sole proprietor until he moved to Kenya in 1974/75. Yohannes remained in Mombasa, Kenya for five years working as a graphic designer, but was frustrated by not having time to paint and determined to move to Europe with the goal of working full time as an artist. Eventually he decided on Germany, which appealed to him for several reasons. His teacher and mentor Gebre Kristos Desta had studied at the Werkschule für Bildende Künste und Gestaltung, a school of fine and applied arts in Cologne, and Yohannes was aware of the school's sound reputation. Yohannes also associated Germany with Deutsche Welle, an international broadcaster whose radio transmissions had been an essential link to the outside world in Ethiopia. From 1980-97 Yohannes lived and worked as a full-time artist in Cologne. Since 1998, Yohannes has resided again in Addis Ababa, where he continues to make his living as an artist and is engaged in the arts community in various ways. He serves as an advisor to students at the School of Fine Arts and Design and organizes artist lectures and roundtables for the Goethe Institute, among other activities. Yohannes has participated in numerous solo and group exhibitions on three continents and his work is represented in private collections in Africa, Europe and the United States.

Yohannes uses no preparatory sketches, but rather works from his subconscious, and does not know when he starts a painting how it will look when completed. He does not title his works so that each viewer will be free to respond in a personal way. His paintings are distinguished by abstract images that often suggest landscapes but with few recognizable forms, or none at all. His fluid brushwork and emotive use of color recall the expressionistic style of his teacher and friend Gebre Kristos Desta and of German and other European expressionists whose work both artists knew from their years living in Cologne and traveling on the continent.

Yohannes' untitled painting from 1967 looks like a wartime scene of conflagration and destruction set in an industrial landscape. He explains, however, that what appears to be a diving or falling airplane—a circular form with wing-like projections cutting diagonally across the painting—is simply a compositional device to divide and define the picture plane. He declines to identify any of the other forms, declaring that they are nothing specific, just part of the composition.

An abstract painting from 1994 when Yohannes was living in Cologne features two egg-shaped forms that he speaks of in terms of parallel universes. The artist feels that abstract paintings like this one are finished when the compositions work equally well in all possible directions, and he sometimes turns the paintings that hang in his house and studio.

Yohannes acknowledges that he was preoccupied with thoughts of missiles and bombs when he painted the untitled canvas from 2003. He chose to reduce the weapons to their most essential forms and to render them in cool, calm shades of blue and white that belie their destructive power. Throughout his life, Yohannes has been profoundly affected by political turmoil and violent conflict in Ethiopia and he follows current events in Africa, the Middle East and the world with avid interest. Often his paintings reflect this passionate engagement with his own country and neighboring regions.

Yohannes Gedamu, born 1947, *Untitled*, 1967, oil on board
5 ft. 3 in. x 48 in. (160 x 121.9 cm.), collection of the artist

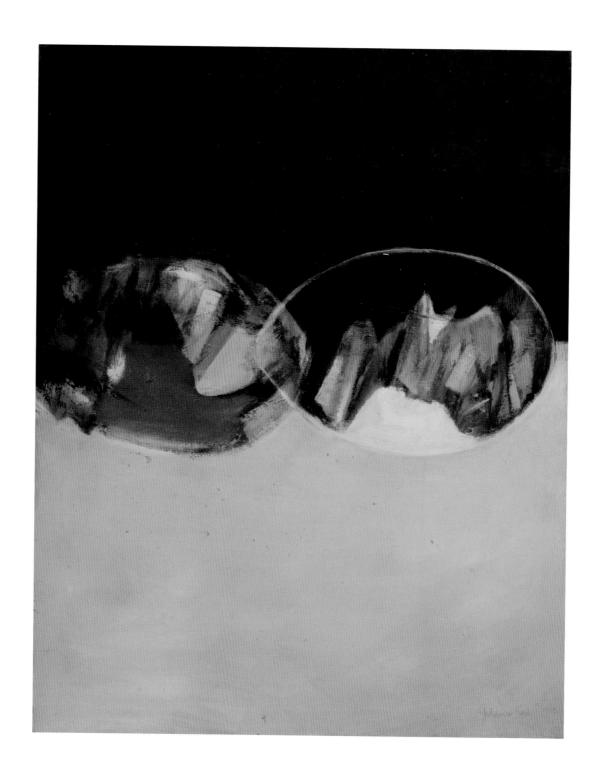

Yohannes Gedamu, born 1947, *Untitled*, 1994, oil on canvas
39 1/4 x 31 1/2 in. (99.7 x 80 cm.), collection of the artist

Yohannes Gedamu, born 1947, *Untitled*, 2003, oil on canvas
5 ft. 7 in. x 15 3/4 in. (170.2 x 40 cm.), collection of the artist

Zerihun Yetmgeta was born in Addis Ababa in 1941. After high school he took painting classes at the Empress Menen Handicrafts School for a year before enrolling at the Fine Arts School, from which he graduated in 1968. Zerihun chose to remain in Ethiopia through the political upheaval and regime changes of the late twentieth century. After finishing at the art school he worked as a freelance artist for ten years, briefly sharing a studio with Skunder Boghossian. In addition to Skunder, Zerihun credits two artists with the greatest impact on his work, German printmaking teacher Karl Heinz Hansen and Gebre Kristos Desta, whom he regards as Ethiopia's greatest artist. Since the 1970s he has taught two-dimensional design and graphic arts at the Addis Ababa Fine Arts School. Zerihun's work has been exhibited in museums in Ethiopia, Germany, Switzerland and the United States. In 1991 he represented Ethiopia in the Cuarta Bienal de La Habana in Cuba. He shared first prize with Senegalese sculptor Moustapha Dime at Dak'Art '92 in Dakar, Senegal, and won second prize at the Kenya Art Panorama at the French Cultural Center in Nairobi in 1993.

In addition to his production as a printmaker, Zerihun has worked in oil, tempera and acrylic paints; pen and ink; and mixed media. For his "bamboo strip paintings" (his term) such as *Wax and Gold* and *Yesterday and Today* the artist glues parchment to bamboo weavers' reeds and assembles the resulting vertical strips into rectangular compositions.[8] The vertical strips are related to the long narrow format of traditional Ethiopian parchment scrolls used for protection and healing. In addition to prayers and other texts, these healing scrolls are often adorned with various symbols and with images of saints, angels and demons. In his paintings, Zerihun borrows imagery from Ethiopian and other African artistic traditions, combining such emblems of historical Africa with images and symbols of contemporary life.

The title *Wax and Gold* refers to a form of Amharic verse with two layers of meaning, the apparent meaning (wax) and the hidden, deeper meaning (gold). Among the images derived from Ethiopian history and art are a stone stele from the ancient kingdom of Aksum, an Aksumite coin, the cruciform church of St. George in Lalibela, and symbolic motifs from healing scrolls. Other African cultures are represented by an Akua' ba fertility figure from Ghana and a mask motif based on Zerihun's study of West and Central African art. An Amharic inscription in the lower half of the painting can be roughly translated as "Don't be a light in a pot," alluding to the fact that the light of Ethiopia's past should not be hidden but rather should illuminate the present.[9]

In *Yesterday and Today* Africa's "Yesterday" is represented by images of ancient rock art, the pyramids of Giza, Egyptian tomb paintings and the Oromo tree of life, a symbol of Ethiopia's ancient past. The central figure of Christ flanked by the twelve apostles represents the biblical Last Supper. The holy figures are surrounded by satellites, space ships and computer circuit boards, reminding the viewer that "Today" religious belief is being replaced by faith in technology.[10]

8   The weaver's reed or comb is used to beat down the weft threads to tighten the cloth during the process of weaving.
9   Raymond A. Silverman, "Zerihun Yetmgeta: Portfolio," *African Arts*, vol. 30, no. 1, Winter 1997, 53.
10 *Ibid.*, 56.

Zerihun Yetmgeta, born 1941, *Wax and Gold*, 1991, mixed media on animal skin and bamboo, 38 1/8 x 25 1/2 in.
Kresge Art Museum, Michigan State University, MSU purchase, 94.24, © 1991 Zerihun Yetmgeta, image courtesy of Kim Kauffman

Zerihun Yetmgeta, born 1941, *Yesterday and Today,* 1993, acrylic, mixed media, animal skin and bamboo
40 1/2 x 47 1/4 in. (102.9 x 120 cm.), collection of Raymond A. Silverman, © Kim Kauffman

Tibebe Terffa was born in Harar in eastern Ethiopia in 1949 and grew up in the predominately Muslim city, which has remained a favorite subject for his paintings. Tibebe graduated from the Addis Ababa Fine Arts School in 1973. While at the school, he organized a group called "Sixteen Young Artists" that met in a rented house after class to read, theorize, talk about art and paint. During the years of the Marxist Derg regime (1974-1991), Tibebe was not active in politics, but nonetheless was viewed with suspicion by the ruling party because his art did not conform to the principles of socialist realism. He was imprisoned several times as a result of negative reports about his work in the government-controlled media. In the atmosphere of greater artistic freedom since the overthrow of the Derg in 1991, Tibebe has been active as an installation and performance artist. The experimental and unconventional nature of his work continues to provoke controversy in Addis Ababa. For example, in the late 1990s Tibebe initiated a project and recruited sculptor Bekele Mekonnen to participate. They focused their attention on a large garbage dump in Addis Ababa calle Koshe Tena, which is controlled by gangs because of the value of trash cast off by big hotels and well-to-do households. An entire community lives at the dump, collecting food scraps to make into soup and various items for sale to the destitute. Tibebe and Bekele talked their way into this community of Koshe Tena-dwellers so that they could collect old pieces of metal and various objects to use for an installation at the Goethe Institute. The resulting work was criticized by prominent artists in panel discussions, lambasted in the press and condemned by many visitors to the show for having polluted the Goethe Institute. In addition to controversial installations and performances, Tibebe is known for the time and energy he devotes to projects with school students, street children and refugee children in Ethiopia and also in Canada, where he frequently spends several months at a time painting, exhibiting and conducting workshops.

Although he has often been at the center of controversy, Tibebe prefers a calm, meditative environment in which to paint. He is interested in philosophy, Zen Buddhism and other forms of religious expression and describes himself as a religious person for whom the process of spiritual discovery and growth is of utmost importance. Similarly, he enjoys the process of responding to something from within that leads him to choose certain colors and mix them on the canvas. Thus for him painting is a form of spiritual expression and may evoke a spiritual response. Tibebe observes that the composition for the painting *Ravens Enclosed* was not in his mind when he began to paint. As he worked the forms of ravens revealed themselves to him. He sensed an element of tension, which is expressed in the completed painting by the strongly contrasting blue-hued background and warm-hued, framed foreground. Ravens are an omen of bad fortune in Ethiopia. When he was introduced to Edgar Allen Poe's poem "The Raven" sometime after completing this canvas, Tibebe felt he had encountered a kindred spirit in the American poet.

Tibebe Terffa, born 1949, *Ravens Enclosed*, 2000, acrylic on canvas, 31 5/8 x 27 1/2 in. (80.3 x 69.9 cm.), collection of Geta Mekonnen

Abdurahman Sherif was born in Addis Ababa in 1939. He studied for one year with Ibrahim El Salahi at the Khartoum Technical Institute, a school of fine and applied arts in the Sudan, then continued his studies at the Addis Ababa School of Fine Arts. In 1961 Abdurahman received a scholarship to study in Germany, where he attended the Akademie der bildenden Künste in Kassel and the Akademie der Künste in Berlin, graduating from the latter in 1968. His first solo exhibition was held in Addis Ababa in 1959 and his work has been exhibited in many group exhibitions, including FESTAC'77 in Lagos, Nigeria. Abdurahman worked as an instructor of art education and graphics at the Fine Arts School from 1970 to 1975. He was director from 1975 until 1992, throughout the Derg regime and one year after its overthrow.

Ghanaian art historian Kojo Fosu wrote in 1986 that at the time Abdurahman had "begun to paint realistic group portraits, which he says are reflective of peasant life-styles in Ethiopia." Fosu observes that "In reality this latest emphasis may be in response to the Government's new direction for art to educate Ethiopians on the historical victory of the masses in the latest revolution, and therefore becoming part of the government's propaganda machine."[11] Abdurahman insists, however, "I was never able to do one socialist work. I couldn't bring myself [to do it]."[12] He used his administrative responsibilities as an excuse to avoid government art projects but was unable to protect faculty and students at the school from such demands. Their work was constantly interrupted by government functionaries requiring they produce paintings, monuments, posters and stage sets with socialist themes.

During the Derg years, Abdurahman had little time to paint, but he used vacations to produce work that he occasionally exhibited at foreign cultural centers such as the Goethe Institute or the Italian Cultural Center. Despite the displeasure of the Derg government, these cultural centers consistently provided venues for exhibitions by artists whose work deviated from the approved socialist realist style. When the Derg was overthrown in 1991 Abdurahman felt that this was "a liberation not [only] for the country, but for me, too, as an artist."[13] His paintings produced since 1991 are colorful, semi-abstract landscapes and figural subjects inspired by church festivals, market scenes and the architecture and life of the city of Harar. They are characterized by warm colors, geometric forms and delicately layered patterns. Abdurahman developed his technique of combining several media in one work during his studies in Germany. In *Sunrise* from 1996, for example, the artist used acrylic paints and silk screen printing on board to create a cityscape with a dense cluster of buildings under a blazing tropical sun.

Abdurahman takes pride in the centuries-old tradition of painting in Ethiopia, which is associated with mural paintings, illustrated manuscripts and icons of the Ethiopian Orthodox Church. By contrast, he points out that in Sudan, where artists make beautiful paintings based on Arabic calligraphy, painting is a purely modern phenomenon. Abdurahman employs this venerable Ethiopian medium to create paintings in a contemporary abstract style, and often with subjects that relate to his experience as a Muslim from a Harari family. *Harari Interior* (1994) and *Water Carrier* (1997) employ acrylic paints and reverse transfer printing on board to develop what at first appear to be abstract compositions. The viewer's eye soon recognizes within the fragmented geometric forms a figure carrying a water jug or a group of women lounging in a room. Although he grew up in Addis Ababa, Abdurahman has strong familial ties to Harar and frequently visits the ancient Muslim city. Behind its whitewashed walls, Harar conceals lavishly appointed interiors with rich carpets, intricately woven baskets and inhabitants clothed in embroidered silks, all in a rainbow array of brilliant colors. *Harari Interiors* captures something of this magical environment, which Abdurahman and his family recreate in the special Harari room of their modern house in Addis Ababa (fig. 2).

Fig. 2 Abdurahman Sherif in the Harari room of his house in Addis Ababa. Photograph by Rebecca Martin Nagy, 2005

11 Kojo Fosu, *20th Century Art of Africa* (Zaria, Nigeria: Gaskiya Corporation, 1986), 182.
12 Conversation with the artist, June 2005.
13 Conversation with the artist, June 2005.

Abdurahman Sherif, born 1939, *Sunrise*, 2001, mixed media on board
27 1/2 x 19 3/4 in. (69.9 x 50.2 cm.), collection of the artist

Abdurahman Sherif, born 1939, *Water Carrier*, 1997, mixed media on board
27 1/2 x 23 in. (69.9 x 58.4 cm.), collection of the artist

Abdurahman Sherif, born 1939, *Harari Interior*, 1994, mixed media on board
26 1/4 x 29 5/8 in. (66.7 x 75.2 cm.), collection of the artist

Born in Addis Ababa in 1952, Eshetu Tiruneh attended the Kokebe Tesibah Haile Selassie I Day School and graduated from the Addis Ababa School of Fine Arts in 1974. From 1977 to 1984, Eshetu studied at the V. I. Surikov State Academic Institute of Art in Moscow, earning an MFA in painting. Upon his return to Addis Ababa, Eshetu taught painting at the School of Fine Arts for three years before taking a position in the Ministry of Culture, where he currently works as Coordinator of Cultural Policy Research. Eshetu's first solo show was held at the Addis Ababa City Hall in 1990. He was a founding member of the Dimension Group, and has been in group shows in Ethiopia, Nigeria (FESTAC'77), Germany, Czechoslovakia, Russia and China. His paintings are in the permanent collections of the National Museum of Ethiopia and the Addis Ababa Museum.

As a student at the Fine Arts School, Eshetu embraced the anti-imperialist ideals that led to the 1974 Revolution and employed an academic figure style for his paintings of working people and the poor. He daringly chose a subject critical of the Emperor for his graduation work, which portrayed the terrible famine of 1974. The biblical themes of Eshetu's triptych *To Live or Not to Live* from 1981 convey his conviction that all men and women are created equal while poignantly expressing his grief over the internecine strife that tore Ethiopia apart during and after the Revolution. The central painting of the triptych shows an atomic bomb exploding over the hill of Golgotha, signifying Christianity, and an Aksumite stele, symbolizing ancient Ethiopian civilization. The artist describes the women in the foreground as the victims—the mothers, sisters and wives who suffer because of the violence inflicted by brother against brother.

On the left wing of the triptych Cain stands over the body of his murdered brother Abel, and on the right wing David looks over his defeated enemy Goliath. The painting is at once a personal, national and universal statement about the reasons for killing—self defense, murder, warfare—and about the victims of violence. When he painted this triptych Eshetu had recently seen a play in which a woman's sons kill each other because they are on opposing sides of a political conflict. The artist observes that the mother is caught in the middle, as Mother Ethiopia is always caught in the middle between her warring children.

The Ethiopians is an unfinished triptych that celebrates the creative and intellectual side of humankind. The triptych also reveals something of Eshetu's method for developing figural images. He first sketches in the composition and renders each figure nude to work out its anatomy and pose, then adds the drapery and details of attributes and setting. He usually reserves the use of a live model for the final stage of painting the drapery. The standing central figure in the triptych is St. Yared, a priest, poet, musician, composer and philosopher who lived in the sixth century. He is perhaps best known as the composer who developed a system of notation for Ethiopian sacred music. Among his attributes are a sistrum and drum, instruments used for church music. The left wing of the triptych portrays a seated but active figure. He is King Lalibela, the medieval architect king to whom design and construction of the Lalibela rock-cut churches are attributed. The church of St. George is visible behind him. On the right wing is Zara Yacob, a seventeenth century rationalist philosopher. He is shown as a contemplative in the classic pose of philosophers dating back to classical antiquity.

Eshetu Tiruneh, born 1952, *To Live or Not to Live*, 1981, oil on canvas, each panel (left to right): 54 1/4 x 32 1/2 in. (137.8 x 82.6 cm.)
65 1/8 x 39 1/8 in. (165.4 x 99.4 cm.), 54 1/4 x 32 1/2 in. (137.8 x 82.6 cm.), collection of the artist

Eshetu Tiruneh, born 1952, *The Ethiopians*, 2005, oil on canvas, each panel (left to right): 39 1/4 x 27 5/8 in. (99.7 x 70.2 cm.)
59 1/8 x 27 3/4 in. (150.2 x 70.5 cm.), 39 1/2 x 27 1/2 in. (100.3 x 69.9 cm.), collection of the artist

Tadesse Mesfin was born in Woldia in the Wollo region of Ethiopia in 1953, but spent his youth in Addis Ababa where artist Lulseged Retta was a childhood friend. Lulseged tells of their days spent drawing pictures of Meskel daisies, which they sold on the streets of their neighborhood as New Year's favors. Lulseged recalls that even then Tadesse loved to sketch from life. Tadesse graduated from the Addis Ababa Fine Arts School in 1972. From 1973 until 1978, he designed costumes and sets for the National Theater. He continued his studies at the Academy of Fine Arts in Leningrad where he received his MFA in 1984. He has taught at the Fine Arts School since 1985.

Tadesse was a member of the communist party during the Derg regime (1974-1991). He explains that he had no choice at the time but the duties assigned to him by the government were not unpleasant. In 1988 he designed stage sets and costumes for the international tour of an Ethiopian folk group known as People to People. He traveled with Korean artists working for the government to introduce them to various regions of the country, where he and they sketched landscapes, architecture and local clothing. Tadesse recalls that in their posters, stage sets and monuments, these Korean artists portrayed Ethiopians with Korean-looking features. His own sketches from this tour, stored in his studio, are a visual encyclopedia of regional building and dress types. Tadesse also did currency designs for the 25 and 50 cent coins. Tadesse was a founding member of Dimension Group. He has had solo shows in Addis Ababa (1991) and at the University of South Florida in Tampa, where he had an artist's residency sponsored by a Mid-American Arts Alliance Fellowship in 1997/98. His work has been included in group shows in Ethiopia, Djibouti, Nigeria, Tunisia, Czechoslovakia, France, the former USSR and China. His work is in the permanent collection of the National Museum of Ethiopia.

After the overthrow of the Derg in 1991, Tadesse felt free to turn from the style and themes of socialist realism that had dominated his art since his student days and to experiment with abstraction and a variety of materials. He worked with different textures, adding sawdust or sand to pigments and gluing string to his canvases. He purchased earth pigments at local markets and mixed them with a binder for durability. He used an abstract vocabulary but included references to traditional motifs and symbols. In *The Gate* (1996) Tadesse painted on rough burlap cloth to provide texture. The dominant white rectangle suggests a gate or doorway, whereas the narrow vertical elements to the left and right recall the shape and patterning of healing scrolls, a traditional art form that has been used as a motif by other artists including Skunder Boghossian and Zerihun Yetmgeta.

During his residency in Florida in 1997/98, Tadesse developed a strong interest in the art of the Ethiopian Orthodox Church and studied manuscript paintings and other traditional forms of art from books. Since his return to Addis Ababa, he has worked with different approaches to figural imagery, bringing together his lifelong passion for sketching from life, his newfound enthusiasm for earlier styles of Ethiopian painting and his continuing interest in abstraction. *Here We Are* and *Three Seated Women*, both from 2003, belong to a series of paintings of market women in which Tadesse experiments with varying degrees of abstraction in portraying the figures, their clothing and the architecture behind them.

Tadesse Mesfin, born 1953, *The Gate*, 1996, oil and mixed media on burlap
35 1/8 x 27 3/4 in. (89.2 x 70.5 cm.), collection of the artist

Tadesse Mesfin, born 1953, *Here We Are*, 2003, oil on canvas, 48 1/4 x 47 3/4 in. (122.6 x 121.3 cm.), collection of the artist

Tadesse Mesfin, born 1953, *Three Seated Women*, 2003, oil on canvas, 18 1/2 x 10 5/8 in. (47 x 27 cm.), collection of Achamyeleh and Connie Debela

Bisrat Shibabaw was born in Addis Ababa in 1965 and graduated from the Addis Ababa Fine Arts School in 1985. Bisrat continued her studies at the Academy of Fine Arts in Leningrad where she received an MFA. During her seven years in Leningrad, she primarily studied the academic style and prescribed subjects of socialist realism. Bisrat returned to Ethiopia in 1995 and worked as a freelance artist until 1998, when she joined the faculty at the Fine Arts School. The same year she joined the Dimension Group, with which she participated in several group exhibitions. Bisrat's first one-woman show was at the Alliance Ethio-Française in 1998.

Bisrat's drawings, collages and paintings since her return to Ethiopia in the mid 1990s are far removed in style and subject from socialist realism. However, the solid academic training she acquired in Leningrad provides a foundation for Bisrat's idiosyncratic and fanciful approach to rendering figures, flora and fauna, and natural phenomena. She is fascinated with vividly contrasting colors and layered patterns. In one group of paintings, for example, she showed women in patterned sweaters seen from the back to reveal their elaborately braided hairstyles and silhouetted against a background of patterned wallpaper.

Bisrat often listens to European classical music while working and finds inspiration and themes for her work in music, legends, folk stories and fairy tales. She is drawn to natural phenomena that are characterized by intricate designs and complex but delicate patterns—the star-studded night sky, swarms of butterflies, interlacing tree branches and flickering flames, for example. The eleven shaped canvases of *Moonlight Sonata* were painted while Bisrat listened to Beethoven's composition of the same title. According to the artist, the paintings of this group relate to Beethoven's music, the sky and stars, beautiful fairy tales and childhood stories. She speaks of individual canvases in the series in terms of shooting stars, constellations, lovers embracing and flying in the sky, the sound of dragonflies' wings in the evening, the reflection of moonlight on the water, the voices of frogs, and the creation of the world. She prefers that the paintings be installed in a dark room illuminated by black light with *Moonlight Sonata* playing softly in the background.

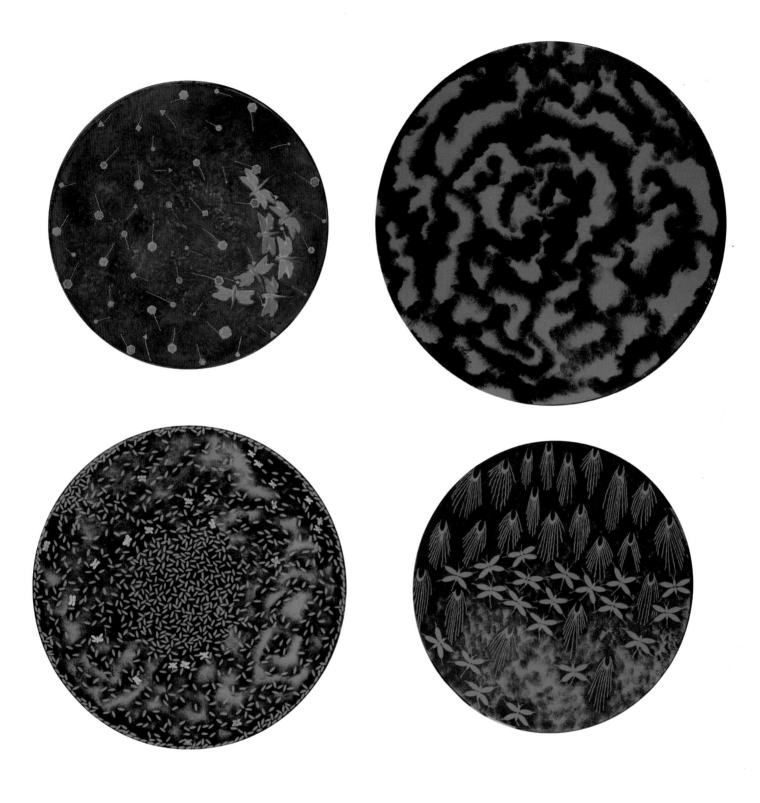

Bisrat Shibabaw, born 1952, *Moonlight Sonata*, 2004-2006, acrylic and fluorescent paint on canvas, dimensions clockwise: 30 x 30 in. (76.2 x 76.2 cm.)
43 x 43 in. (109.2 x 109.2 cm.), 32 x 32 in. (81.3 x 81.3 cm.), 30 x 30 in. (76.2 x 76 cm.), collection of the artist

Bisrat Shibabaw, born 1952, *Moonlight Sonata*, 2004-2006, acrylic and fluorescent paint on canvas, dimensions clockwise: 26 x 26 in. (66 x 66 cm.)
26 x 23 in. (66 x 58.4 cm.), 15 1/4 x 15 1/4 in. (38.7 x 38.7 cm.), 18 1/2 x 13 1/2 in. (47 x 34.3 cm.), 17 1/8 x 26 in. (43.5 x 66 cm.), collection of the artist

Top: Bisrat Shibabaw, born 1952, *Moonlight Sonata*, 2004-2006, acrylic and fluorescent paint on canvas, dimensions clockwise: 38 x 38 in. (96.5 x 96.5 cm.) 43 1/4 x 43 1/4 in. (109.9 x 109.9 cm.), 38 x 38 in. (96.5 x 96.5 cm.), 43 1/4 x 43 1/4 in. (109.9 x 109.9 cm.), collection of the artist

Bottom: The same paintings photographed under a black light.

Geta Mekonnen was born in 1965 in Debre Zeit, Ethiopia. He graduated from the Addis Ababa School of Fine Arts in 1985 and subsequently studied at the Slade School of Fine Art at the University of London (1987-88) and at Bristol Polytechnic (1988-1991), from which he graduated with a BA. Geta returned to Ethiopia in 1992 and for fifteen years has been a powerful catalyst to the emergence of a vibrant and energetic contemporary art scene in Addis Ababa. Geta was a founding member of the Dimension Group, which organized annual group exhibitions from 1995 to 2001. As owner of Tewanney Studio, a graphic design firm, Geta made a personal commitment to ensure that these exhibitions were documented with catalogues. In addition he has built photographic archives of the works of fellow Dimension members. He has organized and co-organized city-wide cultural events including Addis Art Week in 1994 and the European Film Festival for several consecutive years beginning in 1997. He has made documentary films, such as a 2004 documentary for television on HIV/AIDS sponsored by UNESCO. In 2006 Geta received a commission for a public art project in the city of Dire Dawa, Ethiopia. The installation, titled *Rock Art—Living Art*, promotes cultural heritage tourism by bringing attention to ancient rock paintings of the region around Dire Dawa. Geta's work has been exhibited in Ethiopia, Kenya, the United Kingdom, France, Germany and the United States.

In an essay written in 2000, Heruy Arefe-Aine describes Geta's paintings as "provocative questions." He continues: "Geta is interested in exploring what it means to be an Ethiopian artist; a question faced by many artists as they wonder whether to turn to an 'African' model of art, or to work within the Western tradition within which he, and most Ethiopian artists, received training. Should artists be trying to develop a consciously Ethiopian art and what would such a style look like? An Ethiopian urban dweller has a very different conception of art than an Ethiopian who lives in the countryside. How do you develop art that speaks to both?"[14]

Geta has observed that *A Self Portrait*, a mixed media work from 2001, is about "what defines me as an Ethiopian."[15] The work is made up of printed pages from a deconstructed Bible together with a few blank pages. The printed pages signify the old answers to the problems of the individual and society, whereas the blank pages provide a *tabula rasa* for new ideas and answers. Taken together, the printed pages, gun, skeleton and mirrors, one of which is shattered, communicate the sense of intimidation and fear that, for Geta, define what it means to be Ethiopian.

The Hands, a vertical diptych from 2005, also embodies Geta's reflections on the situation in his country. The hands held upward are praying, the hands held downward are begging for handouts. Either way, these hands are not working and are not productive. In poetry and music Ethiopians like to celebrate their country as beautiful, green and fertile, but in this verdant land there are frequently terrible famines. In large measure this is due to the lack of adequate infrastructure for storing and distributing to affected areas the food that is abundant in other regions of the country. Thus Ethiopia's famines are called "green famines." For Geta, this is the irony of Ethiopia, a land of endless contradictions.

14 Heruy Arefe-Aine in an untitled essay in the exhibition catalogue *Geta Mekonnen: Fragments* (Addis Ababa: Tewanney Studio, 2000), n.p.

15 Conversation with the artist, January 2006

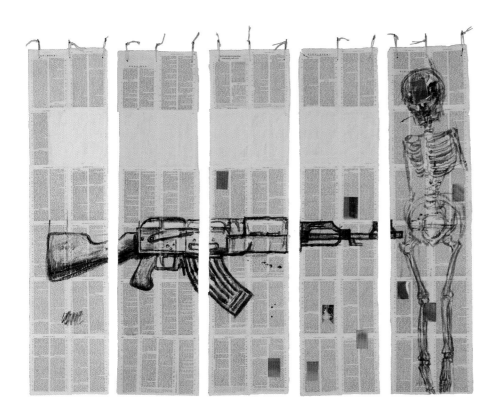

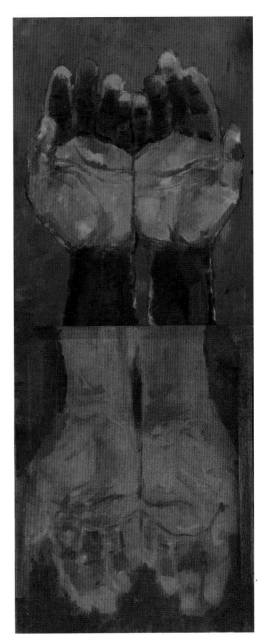

Geta Mekonnen, born 1965, *A Self Portrait*, 2001, ink on printed book pages, mirrors and string
Each panel approximately: 49 x 11 1/2 in. (124.5 x 29.2 cm.), collection of the artist

Geta Mekonnen, born 1965, *The Hands,* 2005, oil and acrylic on canvas, each: 39 1/4 x 31 1/2 in. (99.7 x 80 cm), collection of the artist

Born in Debre Zeit, Ethiopia in 1964, Bekele Mekonnen graduated from the Addis Ababa Fine Arts School in 1983 with a diploma in sculpture. He then taught at the school from 1984 until 1987. From 1988 to 1993, Bekele studied at the V. I. Surikov State Academic Institute of Art in Moscow, where he received an MFA in sculpture. He returned to Addis Ababa to teach sculpture at the Fine Arts School. Bekele served as director of the school from 2000 to 2003 when it was integrated with Addis Ababa University as the School of Fine Arts and Design. Bekele was a founding member of the Dimension Group and participated in the group's exhibitions from 1995 to 2001. His first one-person show was in Kupio at the University in Finland in 1992. Since then, he has had solo shows in Ethiopia, Europe and the United States. In 1998 Bekele was the first Ethiopian to win the prestigious Chicago Artists International Program Award. He had residencies at the Studio Art Centers International, an American school in Florence, Italy (2002); Bowling Green State University in Ohio (2003); and the Maryland Institute College of Art (2006) through the Scholar Rescue Fund of the Institute of International Education.

Shaded with irony and cynicism, Bekele's work is often humorous but with a sharp edge. With his deep-seated pessimism about the political situation in Ethiopia, Bekele observes that the best way to deal with life is to make a joke of it. He is particularly frustrated by the inability or unwillingness of successive regimes to address the most basic needs of the population for food and shelter. Part of a recent body of work that deals with the theme of hunger, his drawings titled *Plows Playing* humorously anthropomorphize the iron plowshares that have been used in Ethiopia for millennia. Writing about a related installation of sculptures fashioned from actual iron plows, Neeti Sethi Bose and Elizabeth W. Giorgis observed: "Known to have been used in Ethiopia in its present form for the past 3,000 years, Bekele's ploughs are curled at their tip indicating a sense of futility . . . Unproductive and yet proud and vain, the ploughs are often found priming themselves in front of a mirror, in battle with one another, leading the crowd or sermonizing."[16] Bekele's drawings of plows and the poses of related sculptures are based on figure drawings from life. He especially likes to capture the poses of boys playing, tussling or lounging on the streets. The boys epitomize for him the all important art of survival. Bekele speaks of the lessons he brought back from his education in Moscow: a solid academic foundation in the use of materials and techniques, a passion for drawing from life (in Moscow the models were retired ballet dancers), and above all, how to survive under a totalitarian regime.

Since the 1990s, Bekele used a variety of materials to fashion his sculptures and assemblages, often purchasing items at markets or collecting discarded materials on the street or from junk heaps. The sculptures *Anger in Hunger* and *Fertility* are fashioned from iron cooking pans or plates. As Bose and Giorgis observe: "He uses the circular form of the iron plate to embody the physical form and essence of womanhood. The use of the darker pigment, the all-absorbing black and the concave and convex shapes formed out of the plates that are normally used for cooking symbolically represent the duality of hunger and bounty."[17] The exploded form of *Anger in Hunger* expresses the artist's anger while also alluding to the fact that desperate hunger breeds frustration, futility and anger in those who suffer its ravages.

16   Neeti Sethi Bose and Elizabeth W. Giorgis, "The critical work of Bekele Mekonnen," *Bekele Mekonnen* (Addis Ababa: Tewanney Studio, 2005), 6

17   *Ibid.*, 5-6.

Bekele Mekonnen, born 1964
Anger in Hunger, 2004, metal
34 x 26 x 4 in. (86.4 x 66 x 10.2 cm.)
Collection of the artist

Bekele Mekonnen, born 1964
Fertility, 2004
Metal, metal filler and marble
32 x 27 1/2 x 4 in.
(81.3 x 69.9 x 10.2 cm.)
Collection of the artist

Bekele Mekonnen, born 1964, *Plows Playing - 1,* 2004, charcoal on paper, sheet: 18 3/8 x 12 1/2 in. (46.7 x 31.8 cm.), collection of Achamyeleh and Connie Debela

Bekele Mekonnen, born 1964, *Plows Playing - 3,* 2004, charcoal on paper, sheet: 18 1/2 x 12 1/2 in. (47 x 31.8 cm), collection of Achamyeleh and Connie Debela

Bekele Mekonnen, born 1964, *Plows Playing - 2*, 2004, charcoal on paper, 18 1/2 x 12 1/2 in. (47 x 31.8 cm.), collection of Achamyeleh and Connie Debela

Mezgebu Tessema was born in the Shoa region of central Ethiopia in 1960. He attended the Addis Ababa Fine Arts School, graduating with a diploma in painting in 1980. Mezgebu received a scholarship to study at the Academy of Fine Arts in Leningrad and in 1989 received his MFA in painting. He returned to Addis Ababa and joined the faculty of the School of Fine Arts where he continues to teach painting. Mezgebu had his first solo exhibition at the National Museum of Ethiopia in 1993. A founding member of the Dimension Group, he exhibited annually with the group from 1995 to 2001. In 2001 Mezgebu was invited by the Japanese government to represent Ethiopia at a conference on African art in Japan.

Mezgebu's meticulously detailed paintings explore Ethiopian cultural identity in a romantic and celebratory way that contrasts strikingly with the political consciousness of Geta Mekonnen's work or the acerbic social critique of Bekele Mekonnen's. Since receiving his training in Addis Ababa and Leningrad during the socialist era, Mezgebu has continued to paint in a realistic style, which he applies to landscapes, figural subjects and animal studies. He makes many sketches and studies in preparation for painting his large, highly finished paintings that reveal the artist's enthusiasm for the landscapes, domestic architecture, farm animals, traditional clothing and jewelry, folklore and religious beliefs of Ethiopia. The untitled landscape from 2002 was inspired by the verdant landscapes of September following the rainy season when, as Mezgebu explains, "everything is so green and lush that you want to lose yourself in the greenness."[18] Mezgebu often paints landscapes from a bird's eye view; in this instance the horizon is so high that the minutely detailed grasses and wildflowers completely fill the canvas. Mezgebu listens to folk and popular music while he works. He associates this painting with a song called, in translation, *Let Me Fly like a Bird* by Alameyehu Eshete.

Mezgebu studied portraiture in art school but has only done one portrait on commission and did not find the experience rewarding. However, he enjoys painting portraits of his wife and daughters and frequently uses them as models. His daughters modeled for *Sleeping Angels*, 2003, which represents for Mezgebu the innocence of childhood and the untroubled sleep of one whose conscience is clear. Another subject of this painting, clearly, is the luxuriant drapery—the traditional hand-woven cotton fabrics with decorative borders that cover the sleeping girls. In response to an observation that *Sleeping Angels* recalls the paintings of the Pre-Raphaelites, Mezgebu responded that he likes the Pre-Raphaelites but especially admires the paintings of Andrew Wyeth. He saw an exhibition of the work of the three Wyeths—N.C., Andrew and Jamie—in Leningrad and has always dreamed of being able to paint like Andrew Wyeth. Mezgebu particularly admires his attention to detail and his scenes of country life. A book on Wyeth rests on a shelf in the artist's studio.

---

18   Conversation with the artist, May 2004.

Mezgebu Tessema, born 1960, *Untitled* (complete artwork and detail), 2002, oil on canvas, 5 ft. 3 in. x 6 ft. 7 in. (160 x 200.7 cm), collection of the artist

Mezgebu Tessema, born 1960, Preparatory sketch for *Sleeping Angels,* 2003, conté crayon and watercolor on paper
27 1/2 x 39 3/8 x 1 in. (69.9 x 100 x 2.5 cm.) collection of Achamyeleh and Connie Debela

Mezgebu Tessema, born 1960, *Sleeping Angels*, 2003, oil on canvas, 41 1/4 in. x 5 ft. 1 in. (104.8 x 154.9 cm.), collection of Achamyeleh and Connie Debela

Born in the Gojjam district of Ethiopia in 1960, Behailu moved with his family to Addis Ababa at age four. Behailu received his diploma in painting from the Addis Ababa Fine Arts School, which he attended from 1976 to 1980. Since 1981 he has been the art teacher at the Bethel Mekane Yesus School, a Presbyterian mission school for girls in Addis Ababa, where he teaches kindergarten through eighth grade and leads the high school art club. Because his teaching career provides a reliable income, Behailu is free to make art however he wants without concern for whether or not it will sell, although in fact his work holds great appeal for collectors. Behailu was a founding member of the Dimension Group and exhibited regularly with the group from 1995 to 2001. Behailu is among the handful of artists living and working in Addis Ababa who have traveled and held residencies abroad. In 1998 he traveled to Paris to participate in a group show of Ethiopian artists, and in 2000 attended Dak'Art in Senegal at the invitation of Alliance Française. His first artist's residency was a three-month stay in Kenya in 2000. In 2001 he spent three months on a residency in South Africa and in 2004 participated in a two-week program in Uganda. The Goethe Institute provided a two-month residency for Behailu in Berlin in 2004 and the Irish Museum of Modern Art in Dublin brought him to the United Kingdom for a four-month residency in 2005. In 2006 Behailu had another residency in Kenya. Behailu has had numerous solo shows in Addis Ababa, notably at the Goethe Institute, Alliance Ethio-Française and Asni Gallery, and has participated in many group exhibitions in Africa and Europe.

Behailu was trained as a realist at the School of Fine Arts. After graduation and especially after the overthrow of the Derg in 1991, Behailu left behind the realist style and began to seek his own way of seeing and portraying the world. Behailu has drawn perhaps his greatest inspiration from the children he teaches, whose fresh and uninhibited form of artistic expression he greatly admires. His subject matter derives from the urban environment of Addis Ababa and other cities to which he travels, including Harar in eastern Ethiopia, Nairobi, Johannesburg, Berlin and Dublin. Behailu is fascinated with the behaviors of urban dwellers and casts a particularly affectionate but acerbic and critical eye on the chaotic and often dysfunctional metropolis in which he lives and works.

On The Street was painted in Nairobi during Behailu's first residency in Kenya in 2000. Like many of his paintings, it portrays modes of transportation in an African city with ironic humor. With cars and a bus in the distance, a man drags a cart holding a bicycle that is ridiculously small for his tall lanky frame. Is he taking the broken bike for repair, or perhaps delivering it to someone else? Who can say whether the motorized vehicles moving through the snarled traffic of Nairobi's streets are more or less reliable than the pedestrian's cart and bicycle?

An untitled work from 2001 consists of four small paintings, each ten inches square. The four paintings were exhibited with twenty-eight others of like size in the Dimension Group's sixth annual art exhibition in 2001. Behailu's small paintings are intended to be shown individually or grouped in grids of varying sizes without a predetermined arrangement. In the 2001 Dimension show the grid of thirty-two paintings included urban landscapes, human figures and animals, modes of transportation and abstract compositions.

The diptych painting with collage titled *DV Lottery* comments on an annual computer-generated random lottery run by the United States government since 1995. Applicants from eligible countries apply for the drawing, which is used to determine recipients of permanent residence visas for the United States. The system functions well for individuals whose education and work experience has prepared them to find jobs in the United States, whereas others experience disruption of their families and lives and are unable to find suitable employment. Behailu's expressive canvases capture the excitement and anticipation generated by the lottery as well as the disorientation and disappointment it brought many of its winners.

Behailu Bezabih, born 1960, *On the Street*, 2000, oil and collage on canvas
28 5/8 x 27 1/2 in. (72.7 x 69.9 cm.), collection of Asni Gallery, Addis Ababa

Behailu Bezabih, born 1960, *Untitled,* 2001, oil on canvas
Each canvas: 10 x 10 in. (25.4 x 25.4 cm), collection of Achamyeleh and Connie Debela

Behailu Bezabih, born 1960, *DV Lottery*, 2001, oil and collage on canvas
Painting 1: 27 5/8 x 27 1/2 in. (70.2 x 69.9 cm), Painting 2: 27 3/4 x 27 5/8 in. (70.5 x 70.2 cm), collection of Geta Mekonnen

Addisu Worku

Born in Addis Ababa in 1964, Addisu Worku studied at the Addis Ababa Fine Arts School, earning his diploma in 1987 in mural art. Addisu was a member of the Point Group, a collective of Addis Ababa artists who exhibited together in the early 1990s, notably with successful shows at the Alliance Ethio-Française and the National Museum of Ethiopia. Addisu's work has been included in numerous group exhibitions and featured in two solo shows at the Alliance Ethio-Française in 1998 and 2003. He is an elementary school art teacher at the Indian International School in Addis Ababa.

Gebre Kristos Desta had already left for the United States when Addisu entered the Fine Arts School. Nonetheless in the use of geometric forms, broad planes of color and bright, pure hues, Addisu's current paintings reflect the influence of Gebre Kristos, the pioneer modernist and expressionist who was among the first to introduce abstract styles of painting in Ethiopia. Addisu's subjects are drawn from his observation of contemporary society and city life, including the activity of people and animals in Addis Ababa's bustling streets. The vibrant colors of Addisu's paintings sometimes belie the underlying psychological and emotional impact of the works. His series of animal subjects, such as *Taming a Horse* and *Runaway*, shows them variously proud and defiant (horses), downtrodden and abused (donkeys), or angry and violent (bulls). Addisu uses these and other animals, including monkeys and sheep, as visual metaphors for the human condition and emotions.

With regard to the painting titled *Philosopher*, Addisu mentions several associations. The man holding and contemplating a skull reminds him of Shakespeare's Hamlet and his famous existential question. While the painting asserts the certainty of death it also affirms life in referencing Ethiopia's role as the birthplace of mankind. Every Ethiopian schoolchild learns about the excavations of hominid remains in the Ethiopian Rift Valley and Ethiopians take great pride in the fact that their country has been identified as the cradle of humanity by paleoanthropologists.[19]

19 The remains of a female hominid known as Lucy in English, or *Denkenesh* (Thou art wonderful) in Amharic, are housed at the National Museum of Ethiopia. When the fossilized bones, at least 3.2 million years old, were discovered in 1974 in northeastern Ethiopia, Lucy was the oldest known hominid in the world. A replica of the remains is among the National Museum's most visited installations.

Addisu Worku, born 1964, *Runaway,* 2005, oil on canvas
39 x 28 5/8 in. (99.1 x 72.7 cm.), collection of Achamyeleh and Connie Debela

Addisu Worku, born 1964, *Taming a Horse,* 2004, oil on canvas
39 x 28 1/2 in. (99.1 x 72.4 cm.), collection of Achamyeleh and Connie Debela

Addisu Worku, born 1964, *Philosopher*, 2002, acrylic and oil on canvas
46 x 28 in. (116.8 x 71.1 cm.), collection of Achamyeleh and Connie Debela

Elizabeth Habte Wold was born in Addis Ababa, Ethiopia in 1963. Her elementary school art teacher was painter Wosene Kosrof, who encouraged her to attend the Addis Ababa Fine Arts School. After studying there she moved to the United States to continue her education. Elizabeth studied graphic design at Baltimore City Community College. She then earned an MFA at Howard University in Washington, D.C., where Skunder Boghossian was one of her teachers. Elizabeth recalls that he painted alongside his students, encouraging them to "just paint" instead of thinking too much about it. Rather than offering direct criticism Skunder got his points across by telling stories. Elizabeth also studied interactive multimedia and Web design at George Washington University for one year. Since the late-1990s, she has worked as a Web and multimedia designer while also pursuing her work in collage and painting. In 2003 Elizabeth was one of ten artists included in the exhibition *Ethiopian Passages: Contemporary Art from the Diaspora* at the National Museum of African Art, Smithsonian Institution. After the exhibition opened in Washington she returned to Addis Ababa, where she has lived and worked since 2001. She is building a body of work in preparation for a solo exhibition in Addis Ababa. Meanwhile, she is still represented by Parish Gallery in Washington, D.C., and had a solo show there in 2004.

When she was in her senior year at the Fine Arts School, Tadesse Mesfin was Elizabeth's advisor. At the time he had just returned from his studies in Leningrad and painted in the socialist realist style. What Elizabeth remembers most about Tadesse, however, is that he required students to make many sketches from life, as has always been his personal practice as an artist. Elizabeth saved her sketches from that period and her studies of beggars are the basis for some of her compositions today.

Elizabeth's paintings are characterized by the use of brilliant color, free and energetic brushwork, and expressive rather than naturalistic portrayals of figures. Elizabeth explains that she uses bright and contrasting colors to convey the intensity of emotions and experiences, whether tragic or celebratory. *Night and Day* (2005), for example, was inspired by the massive turnout for the Ethiopian national elections of May 2005. People stood in long lines for many hours throughout the day and night waiting to vote. There was a tremendous sense of excitement and optimism about the elections and a feeling of hope that Elizabeth had never before experienced in Ethiopia.

In *Tsunami Series I* (2005), Elizabeth uses the same color scheme of intense and contrasting hues to express the horrible events of the tsunami in Asia and Africa in December 2004. The heavy impasto suggests the power of the waves as they catch up and hurl the bodies of helpless victims. Cool blues predominate in *Tsunami Series II*, which shows bodies stacked in neat rows on the shore after the waters subsided.

Elizabeth Habte Wold, born 1963, *Night and Day*, 2005, acrylic on canvas
35 1/2 x 35 1/2 in. (90.2 x 90.2 cm.), collection of the artist

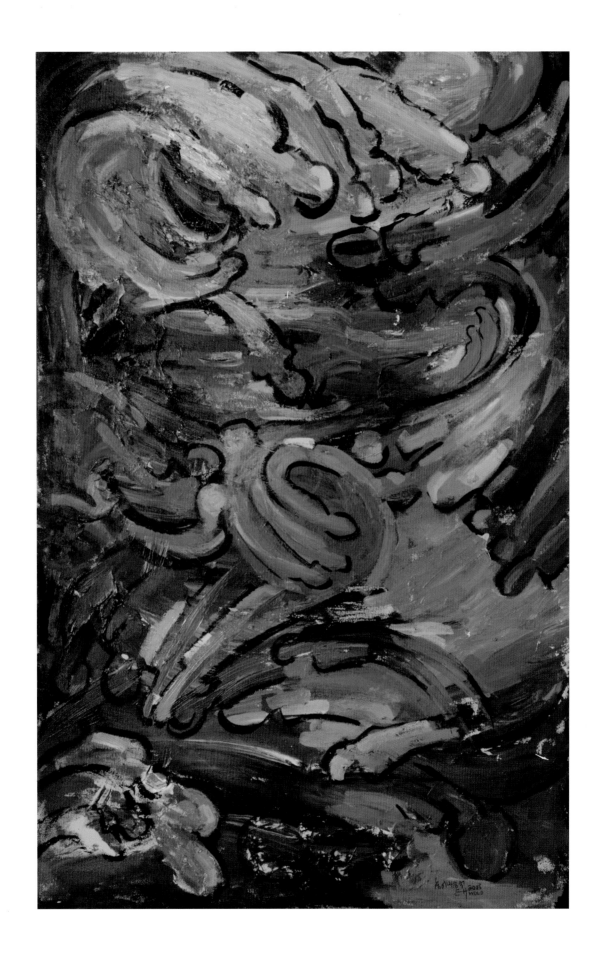

Elizabeth Habte Wold, born 1963, *Tsunami Series I*, 2005, acrylic on canvas
45 x 29 1/8 in. (114.3 x 74 cm.), collection of the artist

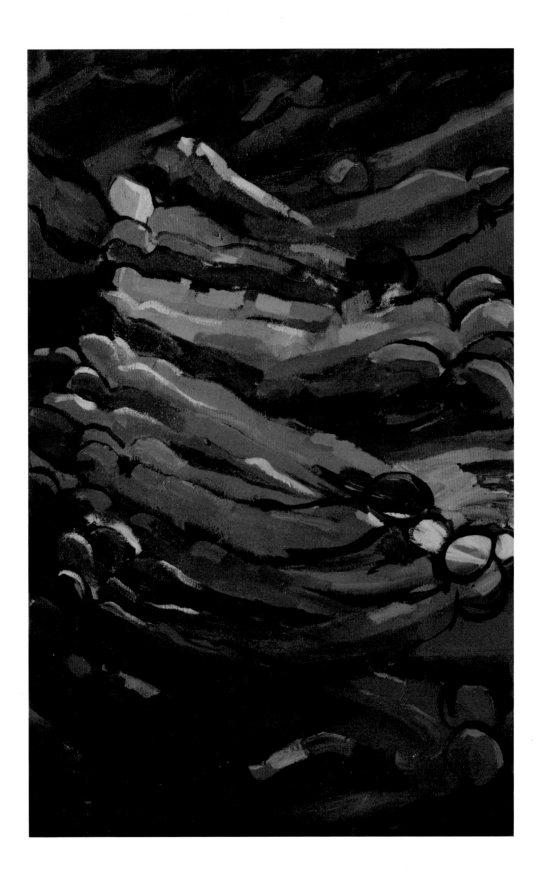

Elizabeth Habte Wold, born 1963, *Tsunami Series II*, 2005, acrylic on canvas
27 3/4 x 17 7/8 in. (70.5 x 45.4 cm.), collection of the artist

Elias Sime

Elias Sime was born and raised in Addis Ababa. In 1990 he graduated from the Addis Ababa Fine Arts School with a diploma in graphic arts, having studied under Zerihun Yetmgeta. Although Zerihun encouraged Elias and allowed him freedom to experiment within the requirements of the art school curriculum, Elias did not pursue his interest in making mixed media works using found objects until after graduation. His first solo show was at the Alliance Ethio-Française in 1993. For several years Elias was sequestered in his studio where he focused on experimentation and art making, only occasionally exhibiting and selling some of his work for income. In 2002 he had a large solo exhibition at Zoma Contemporary Art Center with more than 100 pieces produced during this period of intense and focused productivity. They included large-scale assemblages, wood sculptures, collages and embroidered and appliquéd textile compositions. Elias' work has been represented in a number of group exhibitions in Addis Ababa, including shows at the National Museum and the Fine Arts School among others. He was one of two Ethiopian artists (the other was Assefa Gebrekidan) among twenty-eight African artists in the 2004 Dak'Art in Dakar, Senegal. In 2006 he was selected for an exhibition curated by Meskerem Assegued as part of Peter Sellar's New Crowned Hope Festival in Vienna.

As a child Elias taught himself to sew, embroider and repair furniture. He collected cast-off objects and materials, such as flattened tin cans, and fashioned them into his own creations. Today he still collects energetically, but also pays local children to collect stuff for him—plastic shopping bags in different colors, plastic shoes, horns from slaughtered cattle, for example—and buys some of the raw material for his work, such as buttons, at the Mercato, Addis Ababa's huge central market. In his neighborhood he is teasingly called the "garbage collector." Elias prefers old items and materials to new ones, which have no patina of use. Although he uses garbage and recycled materials to fashion his sculptures, mixed media assemblages and stitched and embroidered compositions, Elias' work is carefully designed and meticulously crafted. He begins his embroidered and appliquéd compositions by making small sketches on paper, then transfers the design to canvas with pencil, and finally stitches or glues his materials to the surface. A single work may require two or three months to complete.

Just as he gathers his raw material for making art from the markets and streets, Elias finds the themes for his work in the streets of Addis Ababa. He does not title his work, believing that titles create barriers to personal responses to his art by viewers. The untitled composition with chess pieces, one white, the other black, relates to confrontation between people of different races and the human propensity for violent conflict. Elias believes that there are no heroes in war and the only real victory is to grow in understanding. In the untitled composition with concentric circles the plastic plate at the center of the design is a symbol for the universality of the need for food and the fact that everyone must obtain food for survival. The hundreds of buttons in many colors represent the people of the world circling the plate, united by their shared need for food.

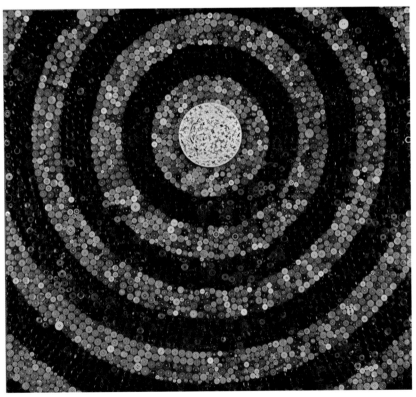

Elias Sime, *Untitled*, 2002, mixed media with paint, buttons and thread on canvas, 52 x 43 3/8 in. (132.1 x 110.2 cm.)
Collection of Mesfin Gebreyes Oda, Addis Ababa

Elias Sime, *Untitled*, 2002, mixed media with paint, buttons, thread and plastic plate on canvas, 52 x 56 3/4 in. (132.1 x 144.1 cm.)
Collection of Mesfin Gebreyes Oda, Addis Ababa

Tamrat was born in 1977 in Addis Ababa and attended the Addis Ababa Fine Arts School, where he studied under painter Mezgebu Tessema. Tamrat graduated in 2000, the year that the school became a unit of Addis Ababa University. With members of his class, including Tesfahun Kibru, he founded the New Art Space Studio at Ras Makonnen Bridge in the Piazza neighborhood of Addis Ababa where he made and exhibited his work for several years. Tamrat moved into a private studio in 2006 using funds from the sale of his paintings. In addition to exhibiting in group shows, Tamrat had an exhibition in 2002 with studio mate Tesfahun Kibru organized by Zoma Contemporary Art Center and Tamrat was given a solo exhibition at Asni Gallery in 2005/06.

Tamrat felt constrained at the art school by the structured curriculum and frustrated by requirements to stretch and prime canvas and make other customary preparations for painting. He preferred to work with whatever materials were readily at hand in a spontaneous manner. In the first years after graduation, Tamrat occasionally produced works that seemed to be indebted to the styles of other artists.[20] Gradually he identified the kinds of materials he wanted to use and developed a distinctive artistic vocabulary with a personal brushstroke, line and color sense that were evident whether his compositions were abstract or representational. For his large paintings Tamrat glues together pieces of gray cardboard—recycled packing material. Used for shipping furniture, the cardboard is salvaged and sold at the Mercato, Addis Ababa's central market. Tamrat uses house paints, sometimes in combination with pastel stick and India ink. He enjoys experimenting with these materials and is not concerned with the permanence of his work. The large painting titled *To Think and Think and Think* is about this process of transforming the artist's ideas into physical sensations, processes and materials. The finished work conveys the spontaneity and immediacy of the art-making process. Tamrat describes this painting and *In Somebody's House* as "time-based," by which he seems to mean that the paintings were "of the moment," emerging from a short-lived set of circumstances and, like the circumstances, also ephemeral. When he painted *In Somebody's House* Tamrat was thinking about the process of building a resumé and about the fact that he never finds time to develop his own. In a sense the painting is a gigantic resumé of the artist's imagining.

In late 2005 Tamrat channeled his creative energy into a focused frenzy of drawing, writing and painting, scarcely taking time to eat or sleep. The result was a new group of paintings on cardboard featuring extensive text passages drawn from his personal journals. The paintings were exhibited in a solo show at Asni Gallery. This body of work represents a new direction for the artist. The paintings are visionary and mystical, the texts poetic, metaphorical and cryptic. The paintings are inhabited by serpents, winged beings, mummy-like forms, flaming horses, rams' skulls and black birds, lending an apocalyptic feeling. According to Tamrat, the untitled drawing included in this exhibition portrays the powerful angel who protects and sustains the entire world and all its elements, animate and inanimate. The body of the angel is covered with eyes, recalling the use of eyes in traditional Ethiopian healing scrolls and the prominence of eyes in the work of several older contemporary artists, notably Worku Goshu. Extensive areas of Amharic script create delicate patterning throughout the composition but are also legible. Tamrat describes these text passages as visual music and as a kind of journey through the layers of his thoughts. Even for a viewer who reads Amharic, the meanings of the texts are obscure or hidden. "Drinkable and undrinkable water can be scooped from the same well," for example, or "Creatures that cannot be cured by medicine can be cured by what they smell, feel and taste."[21]

20 Leah Niederstadt has observed that some of his works at this time used the collage technique made popular by Behailu Bezabih, while others seemed to derive from the work of Daniel Taye, who moved to the United States. She also commented that in producing such works, Tamrat was not alone, as many of his peers also explored various styles and forms, often influenced by their teachers or by commercially successful artists. Conversation with Leah Niederstadt, May 2004.

21 These text passages were translated from Amharic by Achamyeleh Debela.

Tamrat Gezahegne, born 1977, *To Think and Think and Think*, 2005, mixed media on cardboard, 76 x 103 in. (193 x 261.6 cm.), collection of the artist

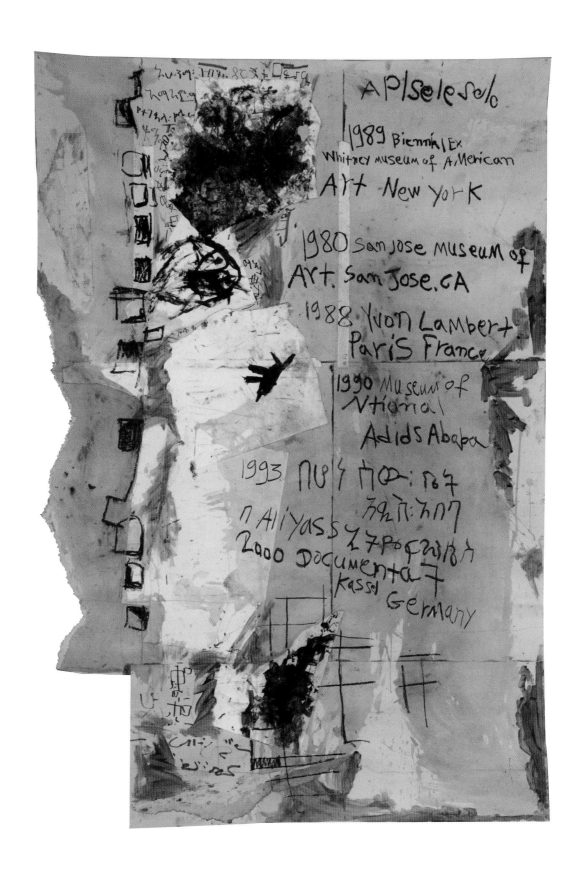

Tamrat Gezahegne, born 1977, *In Somebody's House*, 2005, mixed media on cardboard, 96 x 66 3/4 in. (243.8 x 169.5 cm.), collection of the artist

Tamrat Gezahegne, born 1977, *Untitled*, 2005, paint and India ink on cardboard, 6 ft. 3 in. x 6 ft. 3 in. (190.5 x 190.5 cm.), on loan from a private collection

Tesfahun Kibru was born in Addis Ababa in 1978. He attended the Addis Ababa Fine Arts School, where he worked closely with sculptor Bekele Mekonnen, and received his diploma in 2000. Tesfahun is a founding member of the New Art Space Studio near Ras Makonnen Bridge in the Piazza neighborhood of Addis Ababa. He has exhibited in group exhibitions and had a two-person show with Tamrat Gezahegne organized by Zoma Contemporary Art Center in 2002. Tesfahun has had solo shows of his sculpture at Asni Gallery in 2004 and 2005. In addition to sculptures and installations, Tesfahun designs all of his clothing and has aspirations to design a line of clothing as an extension of his interest in recycling objects and materials. He wants to stimulate his creativity by working with a variety of media and hopes to experiment with filmmaking.

Tesfahun's sculptures are based on his observations of the people of Addis Ababa, whose human foibles, struggles and small triumphs he views with wry but affectionate humor. He uses a variety of recycled materials including baskets, gourds, metal, rubber, leather, wood, clay and, on occasion, his own shorn dreadlocks. For the most part these are not cast-off objects due to the fact that people throw very little away in Addis Ababa. Things are saved for reuse or sold in the markets, so the Mercato and other city markets become Tesfahun's art supply stores. *Surface* relates to the modest clay houses of Addis Ababa's poor neighborhoods. The construction of his assemblage is the artist's tribute to the resourcefulness of his neighbors who build their houses of wood, clay and metal. For this piece Tesfahun bought the wood plane but made the ladder, angling the vertical supports in a nod to academic lessons on linear perspective at the art school.

Tesfahun purchased the leather from which *Skin Matters* is made at the Mercato's special market for skins, a place he describes as "inspirational." He chose the skin for the interesting textured area marking the location of the bull's hump and arranged it to create the desired composition. He considered adding another element to the skin, but decided in the end that the natural form was sufficient. Tesfahun describes his work as a series of discoveries. He seeks to make connections to daily life in his works as he responds to his thoughts and feelings about various materials such as skin. His viewers in Addis Ababa also bring certain associations to the experience of works like *Skin Matters*. Meat is prized in the Ethiopian diet and the skins of slaughtered animals also are valued and used for many purposes, including parchment for the handwritten books that have been used for centuries by the Ethiopian Orthodox Church and for clothing, whether traditional garments of different ethnic groups or the fashionable leather attire of city dwellers.

Tesfahun Kibru, born 1978, *Surface*, 2004, mixed media assemblage on board, 5 ft. 3 3/8 in. x 36 in. x 3 1/2 in. (161 x 91.4 x 8.9 cm.), on loan from a private collection

Tesfahun Kibru, born 1978, *Skin Matters*, 2004, leather and rubber on wood stretcher, 57 1/2 x 31 in. (146.1 x 78.7 cm.), on loan from a private collection

Note to the reader: In Ethiopia individuals are referred to by their given names. A person's second name is the given name of his or her father. Accordingly, Ethiopian names are alphabetized by the given name, or first name.

Achamyeleh Debela. "Gebre Kristos Desta: The Artist/Teacher." In Clementine Deliss, et al. *Seven Stories about Modern Art in Africa.* Paris: Flammarion, 1995, 248-249.

Achamyeleh Debela. "Gebre Kristos Desta: Ethiopia's Painter and Poet Extraordinaire, 1932-1981." *Ethiopian BIR Business and Industry Report*, November 1995, 17-22.

Achamyeleh Debela. "Then and Now: The Arts in Addis Ababa." In Elizabeth Harney, *Ethiopian Passages: Contemporary Art from the Diaspora.* Washington, D.C.: National Museum of African Art, Smithsonian Institution, 2003, 115-125.

Alem Eshete. *The Cultural Situation in Socialist Ethiopia.* Paris: UNESCO, 1982.

Bahru Zewde. *A History of Modern Ethiopia, 1855–1991.* Athens, OH: Ohio University Press, 1991.

Bahru Zewde. *Pioneers of Change in Ethiopia: The Reformist Intellectuals of the Early Twentieth Century.* Athens, OH: Ohio University Press, 2002.

Biasio, Elisabeth. "The Burden of Women— Women Artists in Ethiopia." *New Trends in Ethiopian Studies. Papers of the 12th International Conference of Ethiopian Studies.* Michigan State University, 1994, 304-334.

Biasio, Elisabeth. *The Hidden Reality: Three Contemporary Ethiopian Artists: Zerihun Yetmgeta, Girmay Hiwet, Worku Goshu.* Zurich: Völkerkundemuseum der Univerität Zürich, 1989.

Biasio, Elisabeth. "Magic Scrolls in Modern Ethiopian Painting." *Africana Bulletin*, vol. 52, Warsaw University, 2004, 31-42.

Benjamin, Tritobia. "Skunder Boghossian: A Different Magnificence." *African Arts*, vol. 5, no. 4, Summer 1972, 22-25.

Elizabeth W. Giorgis "The Artist: Skunder Boghossian: Expressions of Specificity and Universalism." *Ethiopian Register*, vol. 4, no. 11, November 1997, 22-25.

Elizabeth W. Giorgis, et al. *Gebre Kristos Desta: The Painter-Poet.* Addis Ababa University: Institute of Ethiopian Studies, 2006.

Elsabet W. Giorgis. "Art in a Changing World: Trends in Contemporary African Art and Diaspora Ethiopian Art." *Proceedings of the Sixth International Conference on the History of Ethiopian Art, Addis Ababa, 5-8 November 2002.* Addis Ababa University: Institute of Ethiopian Studies, 2003, 279-310.

Enwezor, Okwui, et al. *The Short Century: Independence and Liberation Movements in Africa 1945-1994.* Munich: Prestel, 2001.

Esseye G. Medhin. "Addis Ababa Art Scene Revisited." *Ethiopian BIR Business and Industry Report*, vol. 4, no. 2, April, May, June, 1998.

Fargo, Ladislas. *Abyssinia on the Eve.* New York: G. P. Putnam's Sons, 1935.

Fosu, Kojo. *20th Century Art of Africa.* Zaria, Nigeria: Gaskiya Corporation, 1986.

Geta Mekonnen. "Currents of Change." *Revue Noire*, vol. 24, March, April, May, 1997, 36-37.

Harney, Elizabeth, et al. *Ethiopian Passages: Contemporary Art from the Diaspora.* Washington, D.C.: National Museum of African Art, Smithsonian Institution, 2003.

Hassan, Salah M. and Achamyeleh Debela. "Addis Connections: The Making of the Modern Ethiopian Art Movement." In Clémentine Deliss, et al. *Seven Stories about Modern Art in Africa.* Paris: Flammarion, 1995, 127-139.

Head, Sydney W. "A Conversation with Gebre Kristos Desta." *African Arts*, vol. 2, no. 4, Summer, 1969, 20-25.

Heran Sereke-Brhan, ed. *Gebre Kristos Desta, Expansive Pathway . . . Lifetime Traveler: An Anthology of Poetry.* Addis Ababa University: Institute of Ethiopian Studies, 2006.

Kennedy, Jean. *New Currents, Ancient Rivers: Contemporary African Artists in a Generation of Change*. Washington, D.C.: Smithsonian Institution Press, 1992.

Kindred, Wendy. "Skunder and Modern Ethiopian Art." In Paul Henze, ed. *Aspects of Ethiopian Art from Ancient Axum to the 20th Century*. London: The Jed Press, 1993, 129-132.

Kasfir, Sidney Littlefield. *Contemporary African Art*. London: Thames & Hudson, 1999.

Konjit Seyoum. "Ethiopia: The Fine Arts School and the Socialist Revolution." In N'goné Fall and Jean Loup Pivin, eds. *An Anthology of African Art: The Twentieth Century*. New York: D.A.P./Distributed Art Publishers, Inc., 2002, 298-303.

Levine, Donald N. *Wax and Gold: Tradition and Innovation in Ethiopian Culture*. Chicago: The University of Chicago Press, 1965.

Marcus, Harold G. *A History of Ethiopia*. Berkeley: University of California Press, 1994.

Mount, Marshall Ward. *African Art: The Years since 1920*. Bloomington: Indiana University Press, 1973.

Nagy, Rebecca Martin and Achamyeleh Debela. "Adbar and Angel: Evocations of Spiritual Forces in Contemporary Ethiopian Art." *Proceedings of the Sixth International Conference on the History of Ethiopian Art, Addis Ababa, 5-8 November 2002*. Addis Ababa University: Institute of Ethiopian Studies, 2003.

Pankhurst, Richard. *Afewerk Tekle*. Addis Ababa: Artistic Printers of Ethiopia, 1987.

Pankhurst, Richard. "Ethiopian Christian Art: Its Origins and Evolution." In N'gone Fall and Jean Loup Pivin, eds. *An Anthropology of African Art: The Twentieth Century*. New York: D.A.P./Distributed Art Publishers, Inc., 2002, 72-75.

Pankhurst, Richard. *Sylvia Pankhurst: Counsel for Ethiopia. A Biographical Essay on Ethiopian Anti-Fascist and Anti-Colonialist History, 1934-1960*. Hollywood: Tsehai Publishers, 2003.

Sahlström, Berit. *Political Posters in Ethiopia and Mozambique: Visual Imagery in a Revolutionary Context*. Acta Universitatis Upsaliensis Figura-Nova Series 24. Stockholm: Almqvist & Wiksell International, 1990.

Seyoum Wolde. "Some Aspects of Post-Revolution Visual Arts in Ethiopia." *Proceedings of the Ninth International Congress of Ethiopian Studies, Moscow, August 26-29,1986*. Moscow: Nauka Publishers, Central Department of Oriental Literature, 1988, 7-25.

Shiferaw Bekele, ed. *Journal of Ethiopia Studies Special Issue: Tribute to Gebre Kristos Desta and Skunder Boghossian.*, vol. 37, no. 2. Addis Ababa University: Institute of Ethiopian Studies, December 2004.

Silverman, Raymond A., et al. *Ethiopia: Traditions of Creativity*. East Landing: Michigan State University Museum, 1999.

Silverman, Raymond A. *Painting Ethiopia: The Life and Work of Qes Adamu Tesfaw*. Los Angeles: UCLA Fowler Museum of Cultural History, 2005.

Silverman, Raymond A. "Zerihun Yetmgeta: Portfolio." *African Arts*, vol. 30, no. 1, Winter, 1997, 52-57, 96.

Solomon Deressa. "Skunder in Context." *Ethiopian BIR Business and Industry Report*. vol. 3, no. 1, January/February 1997, 14-28.

Tadesse Adera and Ali Jimale Ahmed, eds. *Silence Is Not Golden: A Critical Anthology of Ethiopian Literature*. Lawrenceville, NJ: The Red Sea Press, Inc., 1995.

Taye Tadesse. *Short Biographies of Some Ethiopian Artists*. Addis Ababa: Kuraz Publishing Agency, revised edition, 1991.

Teshome G. Wagaw. *The Development of Higher Education and Social Change: An Ethiopian Experience*. East Lansing: Michigan State University Press, 1990.

Ethiopian Proper Names and Their Spellings

In Ethiopia individuals are referred to by their given names. A person's second name is the given name of his or her father. In greeting, a man is politely addressed as *Ato* (Mr.) and a woman as *Weizero* (Mrs. or Ms.), abbreviated *W/o*, thus *Ato* Gebre Kristos or *W/o* Mariam, for example.

The official language of Ethiopia, Amharic, is Semitic in origin and uses an alphabet derived from the ancient Ge'ez language of Ethiopia. When names and other words are translated into English, several alternate spellings are possible. For example, the following English spellings may be used to refer to the same Amharic name: Afawarq, Afewerq, Afework and Afewerk. In this publication, we translate the spelling of artists' names according to their preferences. For the names of historical figures, geographic locations and other Amharic words we employ frequently used English spellings without diacritical marks to facilitate readability for non-specialists.

The Ethiopian Calendar

The Ethiopian calendar (EC) is based on the older Alexandrian or Coptic Egyptian calendar and is closely correlated to the Julian calendar. It consists of 365 days and is divided into twelve months of 30 days each and a thirteenth month at the end of the year with either five or six days depending on whether or not it is a leap year. The year starts on September 11 of the Gregorian calendar or on September 12 in leap years.

From September 11–December 31 the Ethiopian calendar runs seven years behind the Gregorian year; thereafter the difference is eight years. This creates difficulties when dates in the Ethiopian calendar are translated into years in our Gregorian calendar, resulting in discrepancies in dating by different authors. For example, some historians date the founding of the Addis Ababa Fine Arts School to 1957, others to 1958 in the Gregorian calendar. In this publication we date the founding of the school to 1957/58. The same compromise is used for the dates of other historical events for which there is no general agreement as to which year in the Gregorian calendar should be used, and in the dating of certain works of art.